EVERYDAY DISCERNMENT

Tim Ferrara

Founder of Discerning Dad

Kingdom Winds
Publishing

First Edition, 2019.
ISBN 10:
ISBN 13: 978-1-64590-004-7

Published by Kingdom Winds Publishing.
6 Charleston Oak Lane, Greenville, SC 29615
www.kingdomwinds.com
publishing@kingdomwinds.com
Printed in the United States of America.
The views expressed in this book are not necessarily those of the publisher.

WHAT OTHERS ARE SAYING ABOUT EVERYDAY DISCERNMENT

"Spurgeon said, 'Discernment is not knowing the difference between right and wrong, knowing the difference between right... and almost right.' If ever there was a time for Christians to be discerning, now is the time. In Everyday Discernment: The Importance of Spirit-Led Decision Making, Tim Ferrara lays out the case for how our decisions impact our daily lives, and the lives of those around us. From the movies we watch to our choices as parents, God wants to be involved. If you'd like to learn how to invite God into every aspect of your life, this important book should be on your list!"

Heidi St. John,

Author, Speaker, Podcaster, MomStrong International

https://heidistjohn.com/

"Tim does an excellent job at handling the topic of discernment. He thoroughly and wisely covers multiple topics and how to develop discernment in each of those areas. The discussion questions at the end of each chapter prove to be a useful tool for developing much needed discernment in life. This book is a must read for any Christian who is serious about making well thought out, wise, Godly decisions."

Patrick Antonucci

Founder of Dad Hackers: Becoming the Men God Designed Us to Be

Host of the Dad Hackers Podcast

https://dadhackers.us/

"In a world that is quick to tell you what you need and what will make you happy, Tim has found a way to capture what is truly important in all areas of life...discernment. A life without discernment is like knowledge without wisdom. You may have lots of money, friendships, possesions or charisma, but if you lack discernment, those will all come crashing down or found to be meaningless. In a very concise and transparent way Tim shares what God has shown him throughout his life and lays out a framework for others to follow."

Nathan Bentley

Senior Pastor

LifePoint Church - San Tan Valley, Arizona

Somewhere, between the pages of this book and the pages of your heart, God is speaking - in this very moment. Tim Ferrara calls us to walk in discernment daily, if you need clarity about your next step in your faith journey this book is for you. Tim gives practical steps to increase your reliability on the scriptures and it will encourage you not only to read God's Word, but to faithfully apply it to your life. Thank you for being obedient in writing this much needed message, Tim!"

Rashawn Copeland

Author, Speaker, Podcaster, Founder of I'm So Blessed Daily

www.rashawncopeland.org

"Tim Ferrara has started a discernment revolution! I have witnessed Tim's personal commitment to the exceptional biblical shaping of his marriage and his fatherhood. I pray millions of Christians join Discerning Dad in this discernment journey!"

Rev. Shawn Capozzi

Senior Pastor of New Season Christian Fellowship in Apache Junction, Arizona

C.E.O Ethos Counseling Institute and A.I.M.

"In today's fast-paced, distracted, information-saturated (and opinion-saturated), social media-inundated, hedonistic, and subjective truth culture, it is important, now more than ever, for Christians to be able to discern Truth from 'kinda-sort-a', 'sounds spiritual', 'feels good to me' truth and to know how to live out the Christian life. Tim hits the nail on the head for the need for Biblically-based and Spirit-led discernment and guides us through key areas needing such discernment in this book. This a great resource for a baseline understanding of the role of God's logos (written word; i.e., the Bible) and His rhema word (i.e., the spoken word as revealed by The Spirit of God) as it relates to discernment for the Christian."

Aaron M. Long

Podcaster, Writer, and Founder of "DadInTheTrenches"

www.dadinthetrenches.com

"Lack of discernment, and even hostility toward discernment, constitutes a major factor precipitating decline in our nation. Consequently, Tim Ferrara's book Everyday Discernment provides a much-needed emphasis on this crucial component of the Christian life. Some mandates of Scripture are categorical and easy to apply. However, others require serious discernment in their application. Ferrara points us in the right direction, focusing on Scripture as the ultimate source of this crucial capability.

Especially helpful is his directing our attention to areas of the Christian life where discernment is especially needed."

Paul Brownback PhD, Author

www.truthforu.com

"Tim does a great job of helping readers to make better decisions. If you need help with discernment, then read this book."

Daniel Rhee

Pastor, Author

danielhrhee.com

CONTENTS

This is dedicated to my Dad who has been the primary example of discern-ment in my life and who has shown me the importance of obedience and faithfulness to Jesus.

FOREWORD

The gifts of the Spirit can be some of the most useful attributes to Christians today. But they can also be the most abused.

For those who do not know how to use the gifts of the Spirit, they are missing out on the supernatural ministries God gives to those who believe. It's not magic, or show, or entertainment, but it's God's way of utilizing every member of the Body to build His Kingdom.

Those who abuse the gifts have caused confusion and doubt in the world. I believe God will deal with them in due time. But because of this confusion and doubt, supernatural moments in God's Kingdom have been stifled and many have been pushed away from the Christian faith.

There are few books outside of the Bible that give a clear understanding of how to use the gifts in a godly manner. Tim has done just that in his book, *Everyday Discernment: The importance of Spirit-led decision making*. Although Tim doesn't cover every spiritual gift available, he has taken what I feel is one of the most important ones, discernment, and given an amazing outline of how to better our understanding and knowledge on spiritual and worldly matters.

With a better understanding of the gift of discernment, we all can make better, godlier choices. I encourage every man and woman to dive into this book, highlight the good parts, and start applying it today!

Jody Burkeen

Author, Pastor, and Speaker

Founder of Man Up: Becoming a Godly Man in an Ungodly World

Author of:
Man Up: Becoming a Godly Man in an Ungodly World
Pursuit of a Godly Life
Marriage Advance
Hacksaw Ridge Men's Devotion

www.manupgodsway.org

INTRODUCTION

If you had told me a year ago that I would be writing this book, I would have thought you were crazy. In many ways, the journey to write this book has been taking place my whole life, but more specifically, it started about a year ago with a lesson on the gifts of the Spirit at my church.

Taking a test online, I confirmed that my strongest gift was discernment, which I already could have guessed. It was like a "data download" in my brain during a particular service about the website and blog I needed to create called "Discerning Dad," and I came home and wrote frantically in a notebook about my inspiration for the logo, design, and content, along with a business plan of sorts with short-term and stretched-out goals. Writing a book was one of those stretched-out goals but took place a lot sooner than I had expected. A few months later, it was like another data download about the title, concept, and content of the book, which you now hold in your hands (or read on your smart device).

Working in management for over twenty years, I have seen many leaders come and go, some great at leading and others not so much. The poor leaders I have seen are very reactionary and more passive in their approach. They seem to go to work and put out "fires" all day without planning and being strategic about their routines or the future of their business.

On the other hand, the great leaders I have seen have great routines; they face new challenges with a plan and make firm decisions. Great leaders are the figurative "captain of their ship," turning the wheel in the direction they decide, charting a course ahead of them while being fully aware of the challenges they will face. Those who struggle to lead seem to get tossed by the wind and waves without having a clear vision for what is ahead of them; they make weak decisions without taking accountability for them.

Growing up in the church all my life and now being in leadership, I have seen Christians who are in control of their walk with the Lord. They are strong in their faith and have a purpose and plan for their lives. Even when doubt or distraction comes, they have a battle plan ready to face the challenges. Other Christians seem to get tossed by the wind and waves of life, either leaving the faith altogether or living a low-impact life for God. Many of these Christians have good intentions but have either never been trained on a practical strategy for their new lives in Jesus or have not acted out in obedience to what they have learned.

Usually when I watch the news, I ponder many times why people in general make the same mistakes generation after generation. Why isn't there a manual for how to live that keeps people from experiencing the same hurt and sorrow due to poor choices? I believe the answer to this question is the Bible.

I feel like the calling in my ministry is not to put the focus on me but to figuratively hold a sign with a big arrow on it pointing to the Bible. For the Bible is where we can gain wisdom to understand how to live, and it is by following the rules and standards set forth in the Bible that we experience freedom. The Bible does not only look forward or in the past but allows us to look inwardly and change how we act outwardly as well.

My goal in the coming chapters is to help you reflect on each topic and how it relates to decisions you have made or will make in those areas. I will barely scratch the surface on each topic. In fact, each chapter could be expanded into a whole book of its own, and there is already a wealth of resources out there for all of them.

This book is not meant to be consumed in one sitting. My hope is that, at the end of each chapter, you can analyze what was discussed in relation to your walk with the Lord. The questions at the end of each chapter are designed to be utilized either for individual reflection or group discussion. Pausing to take time to answer them before moving on to the next chapter will help you apply the material to your life.

A goal of this book is to ask yourself, "Why do I believe what I believe, and how can I grow in my discernment daily in my walk with the Lord?" After all, the purpose of having Christian discernment is to test all things in light of the Bible. I would expect no less from you as you read this book. You should have discernment about this book and anything else you read for that matter. If you don't agree with something I write, ask yourself why.

Be open-minded and ask the Lord for insight into what He is trying to tell you as you progress through the content.

It is my prayer that this book is a blessing to you as much as it was to me in writing it.

Let's discern together...

CHAPTER 1:
DISCERNMENT DEFINITION

As humans, we are blessed with the free will to make choices. When we were children, we desired independence but had our parents who helped us with decisions as we grew in knowledge and wisdom. The impact of many factors throughout our childhood defines who we are when we reach adulthood. The blend of nature and nurture gives us a structure for our beliefs and personality and creates a presupposition in how we make decisions daily.

One study estimated that an average adult makes around 35,000 decisions daily.[1] These decisions can be as trivial as what movie to watch or what to eat for breakfast and as poignant as whom to marry and what career to pursue. Many times, it is a history of poor decisions that leads people on a path they never intended to be on. As Christians, our independence that was so fought for as children must be subjected to God. The way we subject our will to God's and make better decisions is through discernment.

Discernment is a spiritual gift, along with many others described in 1 Corinthians 12. God provides every Christian with spiritual gifts; however, not everyone uses them. Christians can specialize in a spiritual gift which can lead them to use it along a path of ministry. They can also be used in specific times at specific places at God's discretion. Unfortunately, the spiritual gifts can be ignored, too, and many Christians fail to move in the power of God that is readily available to all believers.

The Greek word for discernment is *diakrisis.* This describes the ability to distinguish, discern, judge, or appraise a person, statement, situation, or environment. It can be related to the "discerning of spirits" as in 1 Corinthians 12:10 or between good and evil in Hebrews 5:14 (NASB). "But solid food is for the mature, who because of practice have their senses trained to discern good and evil." Discernment is not only a spiritual gift but also has practical applications that are not always based on spiritual promptings as much as common sense built on the foundation of our faith.

I have seen discernment discussed in primarily two places: The Catholic Church and New Age platforms. It's important to note that discernment is explained and encouraged in the Bible, and I feel it is critical for our processing of decisions in life with the help of the Holy Spirit. With this said, discernment should be a

2

talking point more among Christians and in churches today and is a reason that I am passionate about the subject.

I like to personally define discernment as "spirit-infused decision making." C.H. Spurgeon defines discernment as "not knowing the difference between right and wrong. It is knowing the difference between right and almost right."[2] Sometimes, discernment goes beyond our thoughts, feelings, opinions, and faith into the very will of God for our lives.

The gift of discernment may come easier for some as God empowers them through the work of the Holy Spirit. If it does not come naturally, it can be improved on as wise decisions are made through knowledge of the Bible and deepening intimacy with Christ. Discernment can be a process that happens over the course of various life decisions, or it can happen immediately as the Holy Spirit guides. I tend to visualize instant Holy Spirit-led discernment as almost a slow-motion action scene that you see in the movies where you are presented with choices and you receive a prompting or insight on which one to choose.

Decisions made without the wisdom of godly discernment can be successful; we make decisions based on common intuition. We have made decisions our entire lives without seeking God first; we have also made decisions and expected God to bless them. Many poor decisions are the result of not seeking out any wisdom or spiritual insight.

Not every decision we make has to be put through the test of discernment and prayer. Based on the thousands of decisions we make daily, that would be impossible. God *is* concerned with the small details of our lives; however, God has also entrusted us to make wise decisions out of the common sense that He has given us. If we go to God and ask questions like "What should I eat for breakfast? Where should I go shopping today? What clothes should I wear?" we are trivializing discernment and our decision-making productivity will be impeded.

The purpose of growing in discernment is to make wise decisions in key areas for the future and to allow for self-reflection on your past. If you are thinking, "Eh, I'm doing pretty well so far with decisions I have made," that very well could be true. I would, however, encourage you to have an open mind as you read through the different aspects of how discernment can be used and seek God for how you can apply it to your life.

No person will be perfect in all decision-making, but we *can* make better decisions based on the information we have and through the prompting of God's Spirit in us. It's like taking a multiple-choice test in school. If you study for the test and put in the time and effort, you have a better chance of passing and even acing the test. I found that, even when I did well on tests, there were still many questions that came down to eliminating two of the four choices. From the remaining two, I had to choose what I thought was the *best* answer. Sometimes, I was right; other times, I was wrong.

Sometimes, there is not a "right" answer to decisions. Sometimes, it's like the choice between mint chocolate chip ice cream and butter pecan—both are great choices! God is not looking down, tapping His foot, waiting for us to make the "right" decision or punish us when we make the wrong one. However, God does equip us with a working mind, His Word, and the Holy Spirit to help us make better decisions overall. Even if we make some wrong decisions, if we live our lives trying to exercise spiritual discernment and get most of the choices right, we will receive the benefit.

Famous businessman Zig Ziglar said, "If you learn from defeat, you haven't really lost."[3] By recognizing an area where we did not use the best discernment and learning the lessons of that experience, we will be equipped the next time we have a similar decision to make.

Think of discernment as one of our "spiritual muscles." If we exercise it, put it through rigorous tests and practice, it will get stronger. Bodybuilders are not built like they are in an instant; it requires dedication, endurance, perseverance, and failure. Discernment comes through exercising our faith, making a commitment to learning about God, and being aware of mistakes in judgment.

So what are the benefits of exercising spiritual discernment?

In its simplest form, the benefits of not making a bad choice are making a good choice. We know what good choices look like based on our history of making decisions. Sometimes, discernment comes down to making a decision that is in line with obedience to God. Jesus said, "'Blessed rather are those who hear the word of God and obey it'" (Luke 11:28).

Higher-level discernment is sometimes the difference between a blessing and a curse. The Israelites in Deuteronomy 28 were given many blessings for obedience to the law and curses for disobedience. Decisions that we make poorly and without discernment can easily lead to a lifetime of negative consequences. For example, marrying the wrong spouse, choosing the wrong career, substance abuse, breaking the law and going to prison, being in bondage to sin, etc. are usually not direct consequences from God but the result of living in a sinful world and making sinful choices. Many times, we have no one to blame but ourselves for the choices we make and the consequences we have to live out.

It's important to note that, even if we make all the "best" choices available to us, we still will face persecution and trials from being a follower of Jesus. The Bible says that "everyone who lives a godly life in Christ Jesus will be persecuted" (2 Tim. 3:12). This is not a popular topic preached from the stage of churches, but it's important not to forget that millions of our Christian brothers and sisters face persecution on a daily basis.

We also face the consequences of other people's choices not on our own volition. These become reactionary choices once we are faced with a decision (for example, an abusive spouse that we choose to leave). However, many times, proactive choices will keep us on the offensive before we have to play defense. We need to have a "game plan" for our lives before we face decisions, but we also need to be able to call an audible on the fly as situations arise.

Other consequences we face are simply the result of living in a sinful world and make us feel paralyzed (for example, being struck with a crippling sickness or disease). Trying to have discernment in a situation where you feel helpless can lead to frustration. Even in that season, we can rely on God for strength and for insight on how to proceed in areas that we feel we have no power in.

We cannot use this topic of discernment as a way to think that our lives will be that much more prosperous if we make better decisions. I am not trying to present a formula that will make our lives more comfortable. There are many examples in the Bible of men and women being persecuted from no fault of their own other than being obedient to God. Many Christians today are still martyred for their faith.

Sometimes, the blessings that God rewards us for following Him obediently will not come until we are in glory with our Savior.

CHAPTER 1 REFLECTION AND DISCUSSION QUESTIONS

1. How have you heard the term discernment taught within the church or more broadly in society? What are some notable differences?

2. What spiritual gifts are your strengths? (There are tests online for this if you are unsure).

3. What is an area of your life in which you feel you have had good discernment? In what areas are you seeking a greater level of discernment?

4. If you learn from defeat, you haven't really lost. Think about a situation that resulted from poor decisions. What can you pull from this experience for your future or to help others?

5. When, if applicable, have you faced persecution for your choices as a Christian? Why do you think some Christians are surprised when they face persecution?

CHAPTER 2:
HOW DISCERNMENT IS ACQUIRED

Discernment, as used in this book, will not be referring to making "good" choices through only human knowledge. Discernment is defined by having God as our ultimate source of knowledge and how we use the Holy Spirit inside of us as Christians to inspire our decision-making process.

Discernment is not something to be obtained by completing a checklist or improving your head knowledge. Discernment takes practice, and it takes development. Discernment takes success and failure in order to grow. Discernment can be used in an instant with the power of the Holy Spirit and can take a lifetime to refine. At no point as Christians are we flawless in our discernment. We continue to strive to be like Jesus who was the perfect example to us.

Paul conveyed the need to press on to know Jesus and the power He has to offer in Philippians 3:10-12:

> *I want to know Christ—yes, to know the power of his resurrection and participation in his sufferings, becoming like him in his death, and so, somehow, attaining to the resurrection from the dead. Not that I have already obtained all this, or have already arrived at my goal, but I press on to take hold of that for which Christ Jesus took hold of me.*

INFALLIBLE WORD OF GOD

> *"The Bible is a rock of diamonds, a chain of pearls, the sword of the Spirit; a chain by which the Christian sails to eternity; the map by which he daily walks; the sundial by which he sets his life; the balance in which he weighs his actions."*[1]

Thomas Watson

The number one place we have to look to for discernment is the Bible. It is the infallible Word of God that weaves a tapestry of redemptive grace through the history of mankind. Psalm 119:105 says, "Your word is a lamp for my feet and a light for my path." Jeremiah 15:16 says, "When your words came, I ate them; they were my joy and heart's delight."

Do you read the Bible? Is it a joy and delight to your heart? The Bible is a not-so-secret weapon against the enemy. It is the complete Word of God and cannot be added to or subtracted from. The problem many Christians have is that they feel if they have read the Bible before, they "know it" or do not need to read it again. Newer Christians may also feel it is too confusing or overwhelming and don't know where to start.

Hebrews 4:12 says that "the word of God is alive and active. Sharper than any double-edged sword, it penetrates even to dividing soul and spirit, joints and marrow; it judges the thoughts and attitudes of the heart." The Bible is not a stagnant book like any other historical book you might read; it is alive and active.

With the Spirit of God in you, reading the Bible allows God to reveal new things to you every time you read it. If you have read a verse and, suddenly, it takes on new meaning to you personally or invigorates your spirit, then you have experienced the "alive and active" part of this verse.

Knowing the Bible and knowing the heart of God allow us to grow in discernment. We can understand our choices based on the victories and failings of the men and women of the Bible. We can have discernment in relationships based on the example of Samson, aka what not to do. We can see the importance of discernment in our finances and honesty by the example of Ananias and Sapphira (Acts 5). We can understand the importance of discernment with our time by the example of Mary and Martha (Luke 10:38-

41). We can understand why God's model for marriage is for one man and one woman by looking at the life of King Solomon. Just about every person in the Bible is an example to us, good or bad, righteous or sinful.

The Bible is also motivation to us. When we are faced with a challenge or a difficult choice, we can go to it for encouragement. The more we memorize the Bible and can think of verses instantly, the better equipped we are to encourage ourselves and other people around us. We use the verses to aid in our examination of scenarios and decisions we need to make, keeping in mind an eternal perspective of God's plan for His creation.

How can you not be encouraged by verses like Romans 8:38-39?

> *"For I am convinced that neither death nor life, neither angels nor demons, neither the present nor the future, nor any powers, neither height nor depth, nor anything else in all creation, will be able to separate us from the love of God that is in Christ Jesus our Lord."*

The Bible gives us perspective on the past and the future. Billy Graham said, "I've read the last page of the Bible, it's all going to turn out all right." We have the "living hope" that the Bible talks to us about (1 Pet. 1:3). We can use discernment by keeping the bigger picture in mind. We can make choices here today in light of eternity.

RELATIONSHIPS

Another source of discernment is using the wisdom of people around us that God has put in our lives. This could include pastors, parents, mentors, friends, and yes, even spouses. We should never get to the point where we don't need advice from others. We can listen to what *anyone* says, but that doesn't mean we need to follow it. If the advice is relevant, aligns with the Bible, and would be helpful to our lives, then we would be foolish not to take it. English poet John Donne's famous quote applies here. "No man is an island entire of itself; every man is a piece of the continent, a part of the main."[2]

It sometimes amazes me how, over the course of human history, people seem destined to make the same mistakes over and over. If you think about it, there should be enough wisdom out there, enough trial and error, to allow newer generations to read a complete book of "what not to do" (I would argue the Bible is that book). If you just take relationships alone, there have been enough mistakes made by men and women over many generations to write volumes of books—and, indeed, there are volumes.

The reason so many people do not learn from the mistakes of others is pride. Mistakes that are made over and over by the human race are not due to a lack of knowledge on how to avoid them. It's due to our sinful nature (Rom. 7:18) and those that think they have all the wisdom they need without relying on outside sources. Wisdom-like discernment develops over time and with age. That is not to say a younger person cannot be wise. It all depends on how much they seek out wisdom (through the Bible), overall knowledge, and listen to those around them.

If a younger person has godly parents, he or she should take advantage of that and learn from his or her parents' mistakes and successes. Solomon said in Proverbs to "listen my son to your father's instruction, and do not forsake your mother's teaching" (v. 1:8).

When you are younger, many times asking for help and advice is seen as weakness. When you get older, you actually realize that asking for help is a sign of strength. When you understand your own weaknesses and where you need help, you can also better understand what type of support you need. Unfortunately, the more that someone puts on a show and acts like he or she does not need help, the more susceptible this person becomes to growing weaknesses, which lead to bad decisions.

Life can sometimes be the greatest teacher. We, at any age, would be wise to listen to those who have been around longer than we have. It happens in sports; rookies should listen to veteran players who have played through many seasons. It happens in the military; new recruits should listen to their commanding officers who have been battle-hardened in war. If your parents are still alive or you know of older people that you respect, take time and learn from them.

I know that I could teach the younger version of myself some wisdom to avoid pitfalls and struggles. It is no different from someone who has been on this earth longer than we have. I would even say there is wisdom to be gleaned from the older generation not even relating to the things of God. They just know more about how to live and survive as humans. They have had failures and successes we can learn from if they are willing to share and we are willing to hear.

The fact that others are older also does not mean that they will actually share their knowledge with you. They need to be in a position to be able to speak into your life; you can't walk up to an older person on the street and ask him to reveal his wisdom to you. He needs to have built that relationship with you in order for that exchange to take place.

There are times when someone older than you, such as a parent, needs to be cut off from your life because it is an unhealthy relationship. Knowledge and experience do not always equal wisdom. It takes discernment to know when to do this, and it is never easy.

Everyone should have someone to mentor and have someone mentoring him or her. This is important in a career but especially important for Christians. Consider yourself a vessel that needs to be poured into; your mentor will accomplish this role by sharing his or her wisdom with you and helping you through challenges you may face. As you are poured into, you need to find someone along the Christian walk that you can pour into. Mentors rarely jump into your lap. Sometimes, you need to be bold and ask someone you admire if he or she would mentor you.

In the Great Commission, Jesus instructs the disciples to "go and make disciples of all nations" (Matt. 28:19). Making disciples involves more than leading someone to salvation. In the next verse (v. 20), Jesus continues to say, "and teaching them to obey everything I have commanded you." Discipleship is not something reserved for pastors or theologians; it is a call to all Christians.

MARITAL BOND

If you are married, a spouse can be a source of your discernment. I believe that God allows a healthy marital relationship to be a source of encouragement and comfort for us. For the two becoming one flesh (Matt. 19:6), there is a unity of the physical, spiritual, and emotional components. Your spouse usually knows you better than anyone else. It is beneficial to utilize our spouses through open communication when we need to make a decision because they can give us honest and open feedback.

My wife balances me out; she is able to understand my personality and speak wisdom to me based on her love for me and knowledge of who I am as a man of God and her husband. Many times, I have an idea for something, and she is able to lovingly say that she hears my heart but that the timing isn't right. I appreciate this unique discernment that only she can provide me.

Our personalities are a huge influence on our actions. Our ability to discern is sometimes influenced by our emotions or knowledge. I tend to see things as black and white; my wife is full of compassion and empathy. After we were first married, we took a trip to San Francisco. It was our first time there. One day, we wanted to go to the mall. It seemed like a short walk on the map, so we decided to not use the trolley and walk together there. On the way there, we made it to a part of the city that was filled with the homeless. There were no cars or trolleys on the street, and the walk was a long stretch to get to the mall that we had our sights on.

One woman approached us and started sharing her story with my wife. I don't even remember what she said, but she was very convincing and had my wife's attention. As I looked around, we were being stared at by many other homeless people who started to move our way as my wife was having the exchange. I started to pull her slightly toward me, but my wife was empathetically listening to the woman. I sensed a disturbance in my spirit, almost a feeling of dread, and told my wife that we needed to go NOW!

We made it out of there with no problems and arrived at the mall. Now, there might have been zero danger to us; we will never know. I had to help balance my wife in that moment by thinking of our safety, not to say that we should not have been empathetic for those less fortunate than us, but it wasn't the *time* or *place* at that moment.

I tell that story not to claim that one person was right over the other in that example but to say that marriage is a partnership in helping the other person discern scenarios or situations from an alternative perspective. Both parties bring insight to the relationship that can be a benefit if there is open communication as well as reception.

THE HOLY SPIRIT

The last source of discernment that I want to address is the Holy Spirit. Once the Holy Spirit fills us, we have access to the power of God inside us. Jesus told His disciples that "the Holy Spirit will teach you at that time what to say" (Luke 12:12). Paul tells Timothy to "guard the good deposit that was entrusted to you-guard it with the help of the Holy Spirit in us" (2 Tim. 1:14).

The Holy Spirit was given to us for God's purposes and not ours. Jesus, in the book of John, also calls the Holy Spirit the "Spirit of Truth" (v. 15:13), and we are told that Jesus will be glorified through the Spirit's work (v. 15:14). The Holy Spirit is not subjective to our will; we are subjective to His. Since the Holy Spirit is the Spirit of Truth, we can use the Spirit to discern what is true versus what is false.

Jesus promised His disciples that, even though He was going to leave, they would not be alone. "I will ask the Father, and he will give you another Helper, to be with you forever" (John 14:16). The Greek word that is translated as "Helper" or "Comforter" is *parakletos;* it is the source of the English word *paraclete.* This word includes a prefix, para-, that means "alongside," and a root that is a form of the verb *kletos,* which means "to call."

R.C. Sproul, in his book Who is the Holy Spirit[3], describes how a *parakletos* was someone who was called to stand alongside another. It usually was applied to an attorney but not just any attorney. Technically, the *parakletos* was the family attorney who was on a permanent retainer. Any time a problem arose in the family, the *parakletos* was on call, and he would come immediately to assist in the struggle. That is the way it is in our relationship with the Holy Spirit. We are part of the family of God, and the family attorney is the Holy Spirit Himself. He is always present to come alongside us and help in times of trouble.

It is important to distinguish the Holy Spirit from our own thoughts or other spirits. The Spirit will always give a message or truth in agreement with the Bible. We will discuss more on this in the next chapter.

We can properly understand the things of God through the Holy Spirit. There is a big difference between the power of the Bible as discerned through the Spirit versus the head knowledge that an atheist can obtain by reading Scripture. This is a reason why arguing with a non-Christian about topics on which you do not have an equal foundation can be unproductive.

How you view your origins, your purpose, and your future will determine how you live your life.

This concept is described beautifully in 1 Corinthians 2:12-14:

> *What we have received is not the spirit of the world, but the Spirit who is from God, so that we may understand what God has freely given to us. This is what we speak, not in words taught us by human wisdom but in words taught by the Spirit, explaining spiritual realities with Spirit-taught words. The person without the Spirit does not accept the things that come from the Spirit of God but considers them foolishness, and cannot understand them because they are discerned only through the Spirit.*

How does the Spirit speak to us? The Spirit can either speak to us in a loud, persistent feeling or thought, or it can speak to us in a still, small voice. We can commune with our Father in heaven and receive direction for our life. We can also receive words of knowledge for others and for their benefit through the help of the Holy Spirit.

> *Now to each one the manifestation of the Spirit is given for the common good. To one there is given through the Spirit a message of wisdom, to another a message of knowledge by means of the same Spirit (1 Cor. 12:7-8).*

I was at a men's retreat once, and I received a word of knowledge by the Spirit to pray about something very specific for a certain man there. This man wasn't around me, and I tried to reject this thought, thinking it was something my mind created. I walked around the campsite, but this word became heavier and heavier within my spirit. I felt the only thing I could do to relieve this feeling was to act in obedience. I still wasn't sure, though.

What if I went to this man and I was wrong? This is a common fear of anyone who receives a word from the Lord. I put out a "Gideon fleece test" to Him. I asked, if I was supposed to act upon this, to see this man in front of the cabin while I was on my way back (it was already nighttime). I took the short walk back, and, *sure enough*, outside my cabin was this man that I had on my heart. Keep in mind there were hundreds of men at this retreat, and I only saw about a dozen on the way back. I asked to pray over him, and he confirmed the word I had for him was something relevant to his situation.

Now to be clear, God will not always honor our request when we put out a "fleece test." This is an example to show how heavy and loud the Spirit of God feels when He impresses upon you to do something. It is the same with discernment; when we have choices to make, the Holy Spirit can intercede on our behalf if we invite Him into the decision-making process.

Another time I will never forget is when I was on the receiving end of a word of knowledge. My wife was newly pregnant with our first child, our son. I was worrying about the whole process, the safety and health of the baby and my wife, and the whole gamut of questions new parents tend to ask. Plus, I tend to worry in general; it's a vice of mine. A man at church prayed for me. Keep in mind we had not announced the pregnancy to anyone except close family, and my wife was not showing signs of pregnancy.

The man prayed for me and waited. He closed his eyes and opened them, looked at me, said, "Baby," waited a few more seconds, and said, "It's going to be okay." I was blown away. Here my Heavenly Father showed up through information that no one should know in order to comfort me from my anxiety!

Other times, like for Elijah, The Holy Spirit shows up as a "still, small, voice" (1 Kings 19:12). This can only happen if we are quiet and listen to what God has to say. We are really good at bringing our requests to God in prayer but often struggle with listening to what His reply is. God is not a cosmic vending machine! Think about how this would work with your spouse if you just spoke to him or her about your day, your fears, your requests, and then just got up and left the room before he or she could respond? I'm sure you would have a frustrated spouse!

Thankfully, God is patient with us, but we cannot hear what God has to say to us unless we *listen*. Oftentimes, God has to take more extreme measures to get our attention when we create a habit of not listening.

Now that we've looked at how we can receive discernment for our life and situations we face, the next chapters will look at specific areas of our lives and how we can employ discernment to honor God and make the best decisions we can with the Holy Spirit's help and our God-given intuition.

CHAPTER 2 REFLECTION AND DISCUSSION QUESTIONS

1. What are the three sources of discernment as described in this chapter?

2. Ask God to help you evaluate your time spent in reading the Bible. What changes do you feel led to make?

3. Reflect on what interferes with your reading of the Bible. Intimidation, boredom, lack of motivation? How can you overcome these obstacles?

4. How does the Bible help you keep a Christ-centered perspective in your life?

5. What relationships in your life have helped with your discernment? What have you learned from having a relationship with someone older than yourself?

6. Who are you mentoring, and who is mentoring you? If you are neither mentoring nor being mentored, how can you seek out connections to help foster these relationships?

7. In what ways has the Holy Spirit given you specific discernment in your life? In what situation are you currently seeking discernment?

CHAPTER 3:
DISCERNING COUNTERFEITS

My father worked in banking for many years before going into ministry. He would tell us about counterfeit currency since they came across them frequently at the bank. He said that the best way to know if you had a counterfeit bill was not to study every counterfeit bill; you would be overwhelmed with this task since there are so many out there. The best way to spot a counterfeit is to study the genuine, authentic bills. Only by studying the original could you spot a counterfeit. If you are so in tune with the details of what is true, you can easily spot what is false.

The correlation exists with God. Only when we study His Word can we more easily identify when false teaching comes. We do not need to spend time researching all the different religions and doctrines out there for us to be equipped with the tools for discernment. We *do* need to commit ourselves to the lifelong study of God's Word given to us in the Bible and to commune closely with the Holy Spirit.

False teaching has been an obstacle for God's people across all generations. Peter warned about this when he said:

> *But there were also false prophets among the people, just as there will be false teachers among you. They will secretly introduce destructive heresies, even denying the sovereign Lord who bought them—bringing swift destruction on themselves (2 Pet. 2:1).*

There will always be a counterbalance in this world until Jesus sets things right when He returns. For good, there is evil. For true teachers, there are false teachers. For prophets of God, there are prophets of Satan. With just a cursory glance at the range of entertainment media, you see story after story in movies, books, and more of good vs. evil, right vs. wrong, the good guy vs. the bad guy, etc. These are not even "Christian" stories; people have a fascination with justice in a story, superheroes prevailing over evil, many times not realizing the first good vs. evil story is still going on today.

It's usually obvious in movies who the villain is. We know our enemy is Satan, but he is a deceiver. He has always twisted the truth. The hard part for the discerning Christian is that the lie looks so much like the truth, just like the counterfeit bill looks so much like the real thing. It's important to remember, though, that the counterfeit bill has no value *unless* it can deceive someone; the money is *rejected* by an insightful and knowledgeable recipient.

False prophets and false teachings have no power unless they can deceive people and keep them from the truth.

SPIRITUAL WARFARE

Like it or not, as Christians, we are in spiritual warfare. It is real even though we can't see it with our eyes. Many Christians would like to believe spiritual warfare doesn't exist, and they try to be conscientious objectors, not wanting to step into battle and ignoring its reality. Unfortunately, by doing this, they can quickly become casualties of war.

Immediately after talking about the devil's schemes, Ephesians 6:12 explains to us that:

> *"Our struggle is not against flesh and blood, but against the rulers, against the authorities, against the powers of this dark world and against the spiritual forces of evil in the heavenly realms."*

Right after this verse it says:

> *"Therefore put on the full armor of God, so that when the day of evil comes, you may*

*be able to stand your ground, and after you
have done everything, to stand" (Eph. 6:13).*

I often hear the armor of God as a checklist for all
the pieces that we need to be mindful of without the
context of *battle!* Why would you need armor and
weapons if not for battle? What soldier sits in his house
in full battle gear without being ready for a fight?

We will not discuss the specific parts of the armor
of God in depth, but it is important to be aware of as
we focus on discernment of spirits and false teachings.
Many times, discernment in this area is not making a
choice for what is truth but a choice to *fight* against
the enemy! Knowledge of what is true does not win
a victory in battle. A general's winning strategy for a
battle is useless unless it is executed.

The spiritual gift of "discerning of spirits" (1 Cor.
12:10) refers to identifying false spirits, to identifying
persons, places, things that are not of God by comparing them with the Holy Spirit that is present in your
life.

Discerning of spirits does not only mean the demonic, but it can. It can also refer to other spirits that
are not of God, such as a spirit of oppression, a spirit
of infirmary, a spirit of doubt and anxiety. God is love
and truth; other spirits that seek to destroy and bring
dissension in our mind need to be avoided or engaged
with through the Word of God. Someone's personality that is susceptible to anxiety, for example, can lead
to a "spirit of fear" that is not of God. There is not necessarily a demon influencing this spirit.

Regardless of the source of these false spirits, we know the source to combat them.

My parents and I were visiting the east coast when I was in my early teens. We were checking in at a hotel chain that we had never stayed at before. Upon entering, my Mom and I had an intense oppressive feeling in our spirits. We could not identify why. We tried to get past it, to ignore it, but it didn't go away. After checking in, we started to head to our room but quickly realized we could not stay there; the opposition to our spirits was too strong. Why did it affect only my mother and me? What was there in the spirit realm that caused that feeling? There was a conference there at the time; was it some topic that was being celebrated there? I don't have any answers to these questions; however, I remember it vividly as being the strongest sense of gloom I have ever felt. It was different than any sickness and hard to describe, and it went away as soon as we left that place.

Sometimes, the best way to avoid a false spirit is to leave the situation completely!

OUR REAL ENEMY

Christians often forget about the eternal and supernatural aspects of our existence. We go about our daily lives and convince ourselves that this is all there is, maybe not logically but in how we act through our daily grind. We spend our lives focusing on getting an education, accumulating wealth, a career, a retirement, a family, pursuing hobbies...all things that are perfectly fine. However, we are eternal beings with an eternal soul. After we are saved, we literally have targets on our backs; Satan is looking to take out as many Christians as he can before his ultimate punishment. We have to be cognizant of the actions we are taking and the path we are on in this life in light of eternity and God's Kingdom.

Satan, the father of lies (John 8:44), comes at us with just enough of the truth mixed in with lies for it to seem convincing. From the very beginning, he questioned God's Word. "Did God *really* say, 'You must not eat from any tree in the garden'?" (Gen. 3:1). For the most part, Satan will not come at us with traps that we are diametrically opposed to. He will not *usually* tempt the believing Christian with engaging in demonic activities or blaspheming God, which would be vehemently rejected without hesitation. Satan will usually focus on lies, ensnaring us in besetting sin, or sending "Christian" teachers in our way that disguise the truth with pleasant packaging.

Satan knows the Bible and will quote it out of context to get his way just like he did when he tempted Jesus (Matt. 4:6). Satan masquerades as an angel of light (2 Cor. 11:14), meaning that he will try to get us to make small compromises to the Word of God.

Even William Shakespeare in the *Merchant of Venice* acknowledged, "The devil can cite Scripture for his purpose."[1] If Satan knows Scripture better than we do, we are ill-equipped. Only through study of the Bible can we be in a position to discern truth from lies. We can't rely *only* on messages from pastors or teachers or what we read on the Internet; we *have* to be in the Word ourselves!

Another tactic of Satan, through the use of false teaching, is to get Christians to be apathetic about their walk with God. Among the great number of books authored by C. S. Lewis is the highly provocative, although fictional story, *The Screwtape Letters.* In it, the profound Englishman has the devil brief his nephew, Wormwood, on the subtleties and techniques of tempting people. The goal, he counsels, is not wickedness but indifference.

Satan cautions his nephew to keep the prospect, the patient, comfortable at all costs. If he should become concerned about anything of importance, encourage him to think about his luncheon plans, not to worry because it could induce indigestion. And then this definitive job description: "I, the devil, will always see to it that there are bad people. Your job, my dear Wormwood, is to provide me with people who do not care."2

Apathy can strike us at any stage in life and at any area of our lives. But what is apathy exactly? Apathy is an "absence or suppression of passion, emotion, or excitement" or "a lack of interest in or concern for things that others find moving or exciting." We can have apathy in anything from our jobs, schools, spouses, family, children, politics, hobbies, and, yes, even, unfortunately, God.

If we become apathetic about God or discernment, saying, "There's no way to know the truth" or "I'm a pretty good Christian," we become a target and are at risk for being deceived.

We can become apathetic as Christians through what I call "Christian agnosticism." Agnostics believe there's no way to know the truth, so they end up not believing in anything. Christian agnosticism is a casual, apathetic approach to truth and the Bible. Some Christians are bombarded by varying viewpoints from multiple Christian denominations, statements of faith, doctrines, books, teachers, preachers, and beliefs that they end up feeling something like, "I love God; the rest will sort itself out."

It is true that we will not know every detail about the mysteries of God. Many things we have to give over to God. We must understand that we don't comprehend them in our fallible thinking as humans. This does not mean that we should not pursue truth, fight for what is right, and have an "answer to everyone who asks you to give the reason for the hope that you have" (1 Pet. 3:15).

FALSE CHRISTS

The Bible makes it clear that even at the time of its writing, there were different Jesuses being preached. Paul was frustrated with the church in Corinth. He was worried that they would be:

> *led astray from your sincere and pure devo-*
> *tion to Christ. For if someone comes to you*
> *and preaches a Jesus other than the Jesus we*
> *preached, or if you receive a different spirit*
> *from the Spirit you received, or a different*
> *gospel from the one you accepted, you put*
> *up with it easily enough (2 Cor. 11:3-4).*

The Greek word here translated as "put up with" is *anechomai,* which means to endure or to be patient with. These were probably Christians who were in their meetings literally enduring and being patient with false doctrine and a false Jesus. Christians should not have to endure a false Jesus; they should either speak up against it or get a move on to somewhere that speaks about the true Jesus!

Paul again warned the church in Galatia, "But if we or an angel from heaven should preach a gospel other than the one we preached to you, let them be under God's curse!" (Gal. 1:8). The Greek word for curse is *anathema,* which means excommunicated, or banished, or even given over to destruction...talk about strong words from Paul! There is a strong responsibility on teachers and preachers to communicate the true Jesus.

While we do not hear about them all the time, there have been false christs all throughout history, actual people claiming to be Jesus. This seems like an easy thing to have discernment about; however, there have been cult followings for these people. These people believed in what the false Jesuses were saying and did not have discernment about following the real words of Jesus in Mark 13:6 when He said, "'Many will come in my name, claiming, "I am he," and will deceive many.'" Later, in verse 22, Jesus continues the caution saying that false christs and false prophets could seduce, if it were possible, even the elect.

I feel that it is important to give a few examples of this since the only person that comes to mind in recent times is David Koresh from Waco, Texas in 1993. It is even more rampant than one might think. There have been over 1,100 religious leaders in different parts of the world since 1950 who have claimed to be Christ and the Savior of the world. Most of these false christs have risen in Africa, in India, or in the Orient and have spread into the West.[3]

The following are some examples:

One afternoon in 1965, Daniel Waswa, a citizen of Kenya, struggled up a hill and was crucified by his wife at his own direction. As he hung on the cross, he told the gathered crowd, "I am dying for the sins of all Kenyans." After nailing her husband to the cross, the woman collapsed on the ground and died, apparently from shock. Waswa's neighbors knew this was no spur-of-the-moment act. He had talked about it for a year and had told them he had been called by God for this purpose.

They begged him to let them take him down. He refused all requests. Finally, he was taken down still alive, but he soon died from the nail wounds which had become infected. Superstitious people now make pilgrimages to the spot where Daniel Waswa died and pray for him to forgive their sins.[3]

A woman called "Alice the Prophetess" issued "passports to heaven" to an estimated 100,000 Africans who joined her holy war of rebellion against the Rhodesian government. The forty-five-year-old woman claimed she died, went to heaven, met the big black god, and came back to Earth to preach the truth. Then she whipped her followers into a frenzy by standing with her "Twelve apostles" atop ant hills, playing records of the World War II speeches of Winston Churchill. "Churchill," she said, "was the voice of God." Before her capture by government forces, the fanatical prophetess led bloody attacks that caused the deaths of hundreds of Africans.[3]

José Luis de Jesús (1946–2013), founder and leader of *Creciendo en Gracia* sect (Growing In Grace International Ministry, Inc.), was based in Miami, Florida. He claimed to be both Jesus Christ returned and the Antichrist and exhibited a "666" tattoo on his forearm. He has referred to himself as Jesucristo Hombre, which translates to "Jesus Christ made Man."[4]

These are just a few stories of the thousands that are out there of false messiahs and the people who believed them. It is important to realize that it is a real danger to Christians who are blinded by the lies of the enemy and not grounded in having a relationship with the true Jesus.

WOLVES AMONG SHEEP

Some might say false christs are easy to spot, but a more cunning enemy of the Christian is false teachers. They are counterfeits, they resemble the truth, and claim to be from God. Jesus addressed them directly, "'Watch out for false prophets. They come to you in sheep's clothing, but inwardly they are ferocious wolves'" (Matt. 7:15). Wolves tear sheep from the flock, and in the same way, false teachers tear believers away from the Truth, Jesus our Good Shepherd.

True prophets of the Lord faced opposition throughout the Old Testament. Moses tried to convince Pharaoh to let the Israelites go and Yahweh, God, the I AM, would do signs and wonders at the command of Moses. There were Egyptian sorcerers and magicians who would mimic the same thing with their "secret arts" aka demonic activity (Ex. 7:10). They could copy what they Lord was doing to a point; ultimately, their power had a limit unlike God's limitless power. Pharaoh saw this and initially thought that the Lord wasn't impressive if his own sorcerers could do the same thing. Eventually, the power of the Lord was so strong, and Pharaoh had to submit to it.

The same thing poses a threat to Christians as Moses faced. We chase signs and wonders, and many Christians will go with the counterfeit over the real thing. Christians see "power" in things like astrology, new age practices, or other trappings of the occult. They equate this fake power with that of the true God, not distinguishing between the two.

Discernment is also a key word used by new age practices. Discernment is used in the spiritual new age context of channeling spirits, medium practices, trances, and witchcraft. Remember that, for every true gift and movement of God, there is a counterfeit.

THE EXAMPLE OF MICAIAH

First Kings 22 tells a story of a prophet, Micaiah, who stood against false prophets of the king. King Jehoshaphat of Judah wanted to seek the counsel of the Lord before going into battle with the King of Israel, Ahab, to overtake a land they had previously lost to the King of Amram. King Ahab brought forth his prophets, about 400 men, to ask for their advice. They all told him, "Go, for the Lord will give it into the king's hand" (v. 6). King Jehoshaphat was not happy with this answer and asked if there was a "prophet of the Lord" that could be sought for an answer. The king asking this makes it seem like he had *some* discerning wisdom about the fact that the prophets were false; the king seemed to acknowledge the power of the Lord.

King Ahab answered in what I feel is a hilarious response. "There is still one prophet through whom we can inquire of the Lord, but I hate him because he never prophesies anything good about me, but always bad. He is Micaiah son of Imlah" (v. 22:8). Here is the King of Israel hating God's prophet because he does not say what the king wants to hear. In response, the King of Israel has over 400 "yes men" who tell him what he wants to hear. King Jehoshaphat correctly rebuked the King of Israel saying, "the king should not say such a thing" (v. 8).

They brought Micaiah forward with all the other prophets for this "ceremony" of prophecy about what was going to happen with the upcoming war against the King of Amram. Zedekiah was possibly the lead prophet and was a bit pompous in his prophecy. He made iron horns and pulled a "thus saith the Lord" statement saying, "With these horns you will gore the Arameans until they are destroyed!" (v. 11) All the other prophets were declaring victory as well.

The messenger that brought Micaiah forward told him, "look, the other prophets without exception are predicting success for the king. Let your word agree with theirs, and speak favorably" (v. 13). Micaiah responded "I can tell him only what the Lord tells me."

A t the King Ahab's request, Micaiah's prophecy was as follows (1 Kings 22:17-23):

> Then Micaiah answered, "I saw all Israel scattered on the hills like sheep without a shepherd, and the LORD said, 'These people have no master. Let each one go home in peace.'" The king of Israel said to Jehoshaphat, "Didn't I tell you that he never prophesies anything good about me, but only bad?" Micaiah continued, "Therefore hear the word of the LORD: I saw the LORD sitting on his throne with all the multitudes of heaven standing around him on his right

and on his left. And the LORD said, 'Who will entice Ahab into attacking Ramoth Gilead and going to his death there?'

"One suggested this, and another that. Finally, a spirit came forward, stood before the LORD and said, 'I will entice him.' "'By what means?' the LORD asked. "'I will go out and be a deceiving spirit in the mouths of all his prophets,' he said. "'You will succeed in enticing him,' said the LORD. 'Go and do it.' "So now the LORD has put a deceiving spirit in the mouths of all these prophets of yours. The LORD has decreed disaster for you."

After Micaiah prophesied about the inaccuracies of the 400 prophets, Zedekiah (the showy prophet with the horns) came up and slapped Micaiah saying, "Which way did the spirit from the Lord go when he went from me to speak to you?" The resulting verses tell of how the kings went to battle despite the warning, and King Ahab dies in battle just like Micaiah prophesied.

What can we learn from this example in the Bible that is true today about false prophets?

People, especially those in leadership, will seek out advice that meets their expectations, that tickles their ears, and that predicts prosperity and success in all they do.

The true prophets, the ones who preach the full Word of God, the ones who stand for truth will often be outnumbered against those who attempt to deceive. In this story, the ratio was 400 to 1.

Speaking truth will not always result in success or an easy life. Micaiah was not only slapped in the face by the false prophet, but the king had him put in prison for speaking what turned out to be the word of the Lord. We don't know for sure, but more than likely, Micaiah died in prison because the king ordered his guards to not release him until he returned safely, which did not happen (v. 27).

Not listening to the truth, the true Word of God, and not taking action to obey it will lead to failure, pain, and destruction. This may not be immediate, but it will happen. God's Word does not return void (Isa. 55:11). In the case of King Ahab, not listening resulted in his death.

There is also pressure for true teachers of the Word to speak in accordance with the majority. Sometimes, if they speak truth according to the Word of God, they may face ridicule, lose their audience, and/or face punishment.

HOW TO SPOT A COUNTERFEIT

Unfortunately, Christians think they are safe in the "church" from false prophets. Someone that can quote the Bible and can speak the right Christian lingo is not guaranteed to say what aligns with the truth of the Bible.

Deuteronomy 13:1 gave the Israelites clear direction on this matter:

> If a prophet, or one who foretells by dreams, appears among you and announces to you a sign or wonder, and if the sign or wonder spoken of takes place, and the prophet says, "Let us follow other gods" (gods you have not known) "and let us worship them," you must not listen to the words of that prophet or dreamer. The LORD your God is testing you to find out whether you love him with all your heart and with all your soul. It is the LORD your God you must follow, and him you must revere. Keep his commands and obey him; serve him and hold fast to him.

The truth in this passage still applies today. "Signs and wonders" that a false teacher might demonstrate usually refers to miracles. These signs and wonders could have even been from God originally. They could speak truth in accordance with the Bible or God's Word, but *then* they use the credibility they built to get people to follow "other gods."

It's the old "bait and switch" technique. Show the appearance of God's truth, use Christian words or phrases, even quote from the Bible but, ultimately, preach a different gospel. Power, prestige, and popularity can clench their claws into the person's heart, and Satan will use it as a springboard for deception.

While no one can assume the motivations of a false teacher, it is undeniable that power corrupts. When someone grows in popularity because people are attracted to signs, wonders, or false teachings, they *have* to keep the rouse going in order to keep his or her following. Not doing so would be a loss of position, power, and money. Not only that, but he or she frequently needs to "up the ante" and expand the "show" to keep the attention of his or her deceived audience.

Signs and wonders can also refer to power that is not from God at all. There is a deception in place with a misuse of the name of the Lord, a misuse of the gifts of the Spirit. These types of false prophets are connected to the wrong source, not bringing glory to God but to themselves.

FALSE POWER

People who like to play around with the power of God without having a relationship with Him will frequently find themselves a target of the enemy.

God did extraordinary miracles through Paul (Acts 19:11). This was enticing to some Jews who wanted to yield the same power without knowing Jesus. An example of this in Acts was the seven sons of Sceva who commanded a demon-possessed man, "In the name of the Jesus whom Paul preaches, I command you to come out" (v. 13). The evil spirit answered them, "'Jesus I know, and Paul I know about, but who are you?'" Then the man who had the evil spirit jumped on them and overpowered them all. He gave them such a beating that they ran out of the house naked and bleeding (v. 15-16). This is a cautionary story for anyone who is attracted to the works of God without having a relationship with Him.

Predicting the future is not just for astrologers and fortune tellers; many Christian teachers try to dabble in this, too, saying that a message about the future is from God without being connected to the Holy Spirit. Prophesy is a very real gift of the spirit; in fact, Paul told the church in Corinth, "I want you all to speak in tongues, but even more to prophesy" (1 Cor. 14:5, NASB). God has always moved and still moves in the prophetic, but remember that, for every gift of the Spirit, there is a counterfeit. All gifts must be tested in light of Scripture.

The Israelites had a God-given guideline for prophecy as well in Deuteronomy 18:21:

> You may say to yourselves, "How can we know when a message has not been spoken by the Lord?" If what a prophet proclaims in the name of the Lord does not take place or come true, that is a message the Lord has not spoken. That prophet has spoken presumptuously, so do not be alarmed.

Many in the church might like the idea of predicting the future, but the easiest way to spot a lie is if what they predict does not come to pass. This person then loses credibility for any future prophecy unless he or she improves his or her track record. Granted, there is a human factor at play as well if the prophet is not used to moving in the prophetic and hearing God's voice; he or she could be prone to error.

The key to look for is if this person is humble about it or not. Is he looking to deceive? Does he seek to give God glory? Does he push the message aggressively and refuse to be corrected? A true prophet of God or someone moving in the prophetic will not seek glory for him or herself, and he or she should always be humble about his or her gift.

We also need to use discernment against prophecy that *does* come true; it is not always from God. Satan knows certain things and can also use his limited power to even cause things that are predicted to come true, an example of this being fortune tellers that can sometimes predict the future with the limited power they have been given.

WATERED DOWN

False prophets do not always appear with signs and wonders. Many speakers in the church today deceive many others by watering down the message of the gospel to be more "appealing" to the masses. Many times, the reward for preachers doing this is large followings, popularity, and wealth (often private planes). A part of our responsibility as discerning disciples of Jesus is to seek out information for ourselves and make sure what we hear aligns with the Bible. Messages today that dilute the Word of God include:

-Believing in God is all that matters (even the demons believe, James 2:19)

-Removing God's impending wrath against sin (ex: sinning is okay because God's grace never ends)

-A gospel that adjusts to the culture

-Prosperity preaching

-Messages of tolerance and acceptance (usually that overlooks condemning sin)

-Messages of sin that "do not apply today in our culture"

-"God wants you to be happy" (that's not God's primary concern; Christians will face persecution!)

-"God loves you just as you are" (He does but also expects us to repent and change!)

Unfortunately, there are many more deceptive messages being preached today that we will not cover here. A good reminder is from 2 Timothy 4:3:

> *For the time will come when people will not put up with sound doctrine. Instead, to suit their own desires, they will gather around them a great number of teachers to say what their itching ears want to hear.*

May we not be known seeking out what our ears want to hear. We need to commit ourselves to seeking out truth. 1 Thessalonians 5:20-21 commands us, "Do not treat prophecies with contempt but test them all; hold on to what is good, reject every kind of evil."

GIVING GRACE

Finding balance in this area of discernment of false teaching is tricky. On one hand, you want to discern truth as I have been discussing, but the pendulum can swing too far in the other direction. I have been so guilty of trying to analyze every word a preacher is saying and finding all the little "faults" with the message that I completely miss what is being said and how I should apply the message to my life.

A creed many use for guidance in this is (attributed to Augustine but unclear on its origins):

> "In essentials, unity. In non-essentials, liberty.
> In all things, charity."

There are primary (essential) and secondary (non-essential) issues within the Christian faith. Primary issues would cover key "statement of faith" issues that cannot be compromised in any way, things like the bodily resurrection of Jesus, the Bible being the infallible Word of God, the redemptive work of the cross as atonement for our sin, God's everlasting nature, the Trinity, etc. It is important to know what you believe and why. I recommend having your personal statement of faith on key belief points like these.

Secondary issues are debate points many Christians differ in their beliefs. Whether or not you can lose your salvation is an example of a secondary issue. Some of these issues are the cause for the split in different denominations of the Christian faith. We need to have personal conviction for why we believe what we believe. We need to have put in the effort, research, and prayers about these topics.

The Bible says we should "always be prepared to give an answer to everyone who asks you to give the reason for the hope that you have. But do this with gentleness and respect..." (1 Pet. 3:15). We can debate these topics energetically without having to divide over them.

We are always learning, always growing in our knowledge of God. We will never become perfect. We cannot take the stance that we have all the answers, but we need to pursue after them. In the areas of the Christian faith that are purposely vague and somewhat confusing, we need to rest on faith that God is God and we are not.

To know why we believe what we believe, we need to know how some of our ideas got here to begin with. It could have come from our parents, friends, church, culture, etc. To know where we acquired our beliefs helps us analyze whether the sources were legitimate or not. If the sources were not legitimate, we need to reevaluate what we believe in the light of the Bible.

I have heard strong arguments for things contrary to what I have grown up believing. I remember, specifically, a world religion class in college taught from a secular perspective being especially challenging for me and one of the first times I really had to come to grips with why I believed what I believed. Unfortunately, this is all too common with college classes, and Christians who are not strong enough in their faith are often swayed by differing viewpoints.

I have also heard contrary "secondary" issues within the Christian Church to what I had believed. It always makes me look into why people interpret Scripture a certain way or what the history of that belief within the Church has been.

This brings me to the topic of giving grace when it comes to secondary issues within the Church. Now, first of all, it's important to know if the church you are in is healthy and that God has called you to be there, that you agree with the leadership, the direction of the church, the statement of faith, etc. If all that is true, you have to give some grace when it comes to the pastor's message. Like I said before, you cannot be completely critical of every word being said, but you still need to exercise discernment.

People are fallible; they will fail you, they will say the wrong thing, and they will make mistakes. Pastors and teachers will sometimes misspeak, but they also might be challenging your assumptions on things that you need to change. If your pastor is not speaking heresy or something contrary to the primary tenants of the faith, then you should do your due diligence, listen to the message, and research it later. In this case, you should not "throw the baby out with the bath water" and leave the church because of a message you disagree on. I have heard topics discussed in a way I never thought of before. Sometimes, I have changed my way of thinking, and other times, I have said to myself, "That was an interesting perspective, but I still believe what I originally thought."

Once again, prayer and discernment are the key in knowing if you are in the right church, under the authority of the right pastor, and listening to the right teachings. We want to avoid acting *too critical* like we are figuratively raising a number 1-10 over our head at the end of each message on how we would personally rate the context, humor, relevance, conviction, examples, and syntax of each message. Instead, pray. Pray for ears to hear and pray for your pastor and church leadership. Don't engage the rest of the congregation in negativity and gossip!

It's important to note, too, that God is truth; therefore, all truth is God's truth. In other words, you will find true statements from a source whose teachings you should not follow 100%. There are some encouraging Chinese proverbs. I really like some of the quotes from certain preachers even though I do not agree with many aspects of their teachings, and you may find inspiration for your Christian walk from something you saw in a secular movie. God can speak to you in many different ways of His choosing, and He can reveal truth to you in sometimes the most unanticipated of sources!

Our ultimate source is the Bible, and anything that doesn't validate or corroborate with what the Bible teaches should be dismissed. We need to exercise our discernment daily and use the lens of the Bible to provide clarity to the messages we get bombarded with from all sides.

CHAPTER 3 REFLECTION AND DISCUSSION QUESTIONS

1. What counterfeit teachings have you seen in the Christian Church?

2. What is an example of spiritual warfare in your life with which you have been engaged, and how did you overcome it?

3. How do you see apathy as a tool used by Satan to keep Christians from action? How can we combat it within ourselves and help others overcome it as well?

4. How are false christs and false teachers able to deceive so many? How as Christians can we stay on guard against this?

5. Have you ever stood in the minority for God like in the example of the prophet Micaiah? Explain.

6. What are some deceptive "signs and wonders" in the world today that people attribute to God?

7. What are some primary and secondary issues in the Christian Church today? Why is it important to give grace to Christians on secondary issues?

8. In what ways have you been so critical of a sermon that you missed the point of the message? How can you balance being wise against false teaching but also being open to learning something new?

CHAPTER 4:
DISCERNMENT OF SIN

Why is discernment important when facing sin and temptation? After all, when faced with a choice, the Christian must simply *choose* not to sin, right? We know it is not this easy. Why is it not always an easy decision, and how can we resist temptation? We will start with a definition of sin.

DEFINITION OF SIN

Sin can be defined as "transgression of God's will, either by doing what He forbids, or failing to do what He requires." Sin came into the world through one man, Adam, and death through sin came to all people because all have sinned (Rom. 5:12). We are forgiven of our sinful past when we repent and decide to follow Jesus.

For since the creation of the world God's invisible qualities--his eternal power and divine nature--have been clearly seen, being understood from what has been made, so that people are without excuse (Rom. 1:20).

Romans makes it clear that everyone is without excuse from knowing there is a God. This is similar to being pulled over by law enforcement for breaking a law; not knowing the law does not abstain us from the consequences. However, just like a judge who does not send a convicted man to prison but instead goes to prison in his place, Jesus took the place for our sin on the cross and bore the punishment so that we do not have to, so that we can have an eternal life with Him.

Sin can also be defined in James 4:7. "If anyone then, knows the good they ought to do and doesn't do it, it is sin for them." The more we learn and grow as Christians, the more we are held accountable to our knowledge, but with that knowledge, we have more tools to resist sin with the help of the Holy Spirit.

CHRISTIAN GROWTH

Accepting Jesus as our Lord and Savior is the starting line for the Christian race. Hebrews alludes to this race when it says, "Let us run with perseverance the race marked out for us, fixing our eyes on Jesus, the pioneer and perfecter of faith" (v. 12:1-2). It's important to note that Christians will all be at various stages of this race.

Newer Christians will frequently take time to grow and mature in their faith. Paul talks in 1 Corinthians about Christians who were "still worldly--mere infants in Christ" (v. 3:1) and how he gave them milk and not solid food because they were not ready for it (v. 3:2). Growth is not a guaranteed thing in the Christian walk. The person needs to make a conscious effort to learn, grow, pray, read the Bible, listen to God, etc. in order to make steps in the right direction.

Too often, Christians will look at other Christians and compare themselves to one another. They will compare their sins and think, "Well, at least I'm not (fill in the blank)." This creates a false self-righteousness in our own mind and is a dangerous game to play. We get this mentality in our self-preservation as humans.

From an early age, we start this comparison with those around us, and it just grows into adulthood. We compare toys with other kids, clothing with our friends, social statuses, the cars we drive, the parents we have or do not have, the colleges we attend, the spouses we have, the behavior of our kids, and unfortunately, the sin in other people's lives.

Jesus addressed this in Matthew 7:3 when He said to the crowd at the Sermon on the Mount, "'Why do you look at the speck of sawdust in your brother's eye and pay no attention to the plank in your own eye?'" If we spend our time in the Church comparing ourselves to those we feel are not as "holy" as we are and not evaluating the sin in our own lives, we are deceived, we are not put in a position of integrity, and we end up being hypocrites. Jesus condemned the Pharisees for being "whitewashed tombs," saying they "clean the outside of the cup and dish, but inside they are full of greed and self-indulgence" (Matt. 23:25, 27).

We need to give grace to our brothers and sisters in Christ while focusing on ourselves first but also call out the sin if we have positioned ourselves in having a relationship with them. We cannot speak into the lives of another person without first loving him more than hating his sin. If we understand that Christians are at all stages of the "race," we must pray that the Holy Spirit will reveal to them the areas where they need to cleanse their sin, but we must not gossip about it or try to do the Holy Spirit's job of conviction (1 John 16:8).

IS PERFECTION THE GOAL?

Perfection is impossible to achieve, bottom line. The only person who never sinned was Jesus (Heb. 4:15). He lived a flawless life, completely innocent of any sin. We are commanded to follow His example, but we cannot attain perfection (1 John 1:8).

The legendary football coach Vince Lombardi is said to have told his Green Bay Packers: "Perfection is not attainable, but if we chase perfection, we can catch excellence."

Charles Spurgeon wrote, "I believe the holier a man becomes the more he mourns over the unholiness which remains in him."[1]

Paul expressed his desire to "be like Christ," but for as much as Paul achieved in his life, he still stated, "Not that I have already achieved these things or that I have already reached perfection. But I press on to possess that perfection for which Christ Jesus first possessed me" (Phil. 3:12, NLT).

Not being able to reach perfection does not mean we should not even try; that's like saying, if I can't win the Super Bowl, I'm not even going to play the game. If we are stuck as Christians on "milk messages," living in sin and bondage, and not submitting to God's will, we lose out on the freedom that Jesus offers us when we are growing in a relationship with Him and living for Him.

"Now the Lord is the Spirit, and where the Spirit of the Lord is, there is freedom" (2 Cor. 3:17), "but do not use your freedom to indulge the flesh; rather, serve one another humbly in love" (Gal. 5:13). We experience true freedom, not when we follow our rules but when we live in obedience to God's rules. God knows what is best for us and how His creation should live; if we submit ourselves to His plan, we find the true reason for our whole existence... to worship and serve our Creator!

It's no different with the rules parents give their children, things like: don't run into the street, don't eat candy for breakfast, don't take candy from strangers, don't spend all of your money on toys, don't hit your sibling, etc. The rules are not designed for the purpose of limiting their fun and freedom, but they are designed out of love with the child's protection in mind, an understanding of his or her limitations, and an awareness of the dangers he or she may face.

Children are usually oblivious to the dangers in the world; they need to rely on their parents for direction. Christians as well can be oblivious to the dangers both in the physical and spiritual world. Christians need to walk in obedience and rely on the guidelines given by God in order to experience true freedom.

The rules are designed in sports for a reason. The players on a football field are given the freedom to enjoy the game and be successful if they follow the specific rules. Sports games without rules would result in complete chaos, not being fun for the players or the fans.

STAGES OF SIN

Augustine is said to have stated 3 stages to sin in his life:

1. Lord make me good, but not yet.

2. Lord make me good, but not entirely.

3. Lord make me good (Source Unknown).

These are important to understand as we run the race and grow in our relationship with Jesus. Some Christians start off with salvation and on fire for God. Other Christians start slower, not wanting to give up their old lives filled with vices. We then transition to giving over certain aspects of our lives to God but hold on tightly to other areas. Examples of this could be finances or a besetting sin we do not want to release. Finally, as the Holy Spirit has His way in us, we release everything to God and strive for holiness at any cost.

These are not the stages for *every* Christian, and some Christians will progress through them faster than others, but I feel they are important to understand. The sooner we can grow, develop, and mature in the Lord, the closer we are to Him and the fewer consequences we have to face for our mistakes.

The Bible tells us the consequences of sin is death (Rom. 6:23). This death is often believed to only be after we die; however, if we look at sin while we are Christians, it separates us from a relationship with God with our burden of guilt; it keeps the Holy Spirit from living comfortably in our lives.

The dangerous cycle of sin is designed by our enemy to keep us from growing in our relationships with God. This is what the sin cycle looks like... We sin, we may or may not repent, we feel separated from God, and due to this feeling of separation, we are susceptible to committing the same sin again and again. After we sin, we should turn to God, read the Bible, pray, and find accountability to turn away from the sin cycle.

However, it is very hard to do because of the "feelings of separation" from God. We feel ashamed, confused, frustrated, weak, helpless, and like God would never forgive us. These feelings do not equate to the reality of how God feels about us. He is waiting for us to return to Him, confess, and turn from our sin for good. God desires relationship with His creation.

Paul writes about this struggle with our sinful nature in Romans 7:14-25:

> We know that the law is spiritual; but I am unspiritual, sold as a slave to sin. I do not understand what I do. For what I want to do I do not do, but what I hate I do. And if I do what I do not want to do, I agree that the law is good. As it is, it is no longer I myself who do it, but it is sin living in me. For I know that good itself does not dwell in me, that is, in my sinful nature. For I have the desire to do what is good, but I cannot carry it out. For I do not do the good I want to do, but the evil I do not want to do—this I keep on doing.
>
> Now if I do what I do not want to do, it is no longer I who do it, but it is sin living in me that does it. So I find this law at work: Although I want to do good, evil is right there with me. For in my inner being I delight in God's law; but I see another law at work in me, waging war against the law of my mind and making me a prisoner of the law of sin at work within me. What a wretched man I am! Who will rescue me from this body that

is subject to death? Thanks be to God, who delivers me through Jesus Christ our Lord!

The sin cycle is not something that can be overcome by our own will or persistence because it is human nature that keeps us sinning! Only through a renewing of our mind and an overhaul in our nature by trying to be more like Jesus can we overcome this cycle. Not that we will achieve perfection but that sin will not control us and we will know how to quickly move back to safety when we slip up again. We should view sin as a hindrance, an annoyance, and hate the sin that keeps us from a relationship with our Heavenly Father. If we place a higher value on the sin instead of a relationship with Jesus, it makes the sin more tempting.

I have heard it said that "a familiar captivity is frequently more desirable than an unfamiliar freedom." People often choose sin because it's familiar. It's like when you move to a new home; it doesn't *feel* like home for a while. When you go back to visit your old property, you think back to the memories that were created there and it feels comfortable. You know the ins and outs of that place. Eventually, though, you create a new identity in your new house, and over time, we create a new identity in Jesus.

OVERCOMING SIN

God told Cain that, "'If you do not do what is right, sin is crouching at the door; it desires to have you, but you must rule over it'" (Gen. 4:7). Cain had a warning. God gave him a way out. Cain chose not to heed the warning and, instead, killed his brother. Sin is always a choice. It can be a very hard choice. It can feel like we are powerless against making the choice, but it is a choice, nonetheless.

It is crucial that we use discernment when faced with a choice to sin (remember that we get discernment from the Bible, Godly relationships, and the Holy Spirit). Sin is figuratively crouching at the door waiting to be let in. Sometimes, the temptation to sin will never go away completely, but the less that we entertain sin by letting it enter our spiritual home, the more comfortable we are in combatting it.

Have you been stuck or are you stuck in a sinful lifestyle or action that feels so "at home" to you that you could not imagine your life without it? You know it is wrong, but you don't know what you would do without the feelings it brings you, the friends it gets you, or the attention that comes your way. This is the "fowler's snare" (Psalm 91:3) that the Bible talks about relating to sin and the tricks of Satan. A snare is laid to be invisible to its prey. We may know it is coming or that it is close by, but before we know it, it captures us. We must avoid the area completely! We may not know exactly where the trap is, but we know the general vicinity.

Too many Christians feel they can dabble in the appearance of sin and that they can stop at any point that they want. We think we are safe in the shallow water of sin, just taking a dip, and that we can get back safely to shore whenever we want. But too often, a giant wave will come and pull us out into the open water, and then we are trapped, struggling to swim back.

An example of this applies to the alcoholic who thinks they can have "just a few drinks; I can stop at any point." This is a cautionary tale for someone struggling with lust who thinks they can "take a second glance." This is a word of warning for someone who has a struggle with anger and lets uncontrolled thoughts enter his heart and mind. Watch out that you do not compare levels of sin as someone who loves to gossip convinces herself, "I'm only telling my best friend; she won't tell anyone." Do you see how small compromises of sin can lead to a full-blown addiction?

Too often, Christians hate the sin in other people's lives more than they hate the sin in their own!

If we surround ourselves with God on a daily, even hourly, basis by praying and reading the Bible, we feel more equipped to combat sin when it seeks to enter our homes. We *personally* know where our struggle lies. My struggle with sin will be different than yours. We need to be aware of where we are weak so we can let Jesus in His strength lead us through those areas of weakness. We need to discern in that moment of weakness what choices we have and pick the one that leads to life instead of death.

Surrounding ourselves with others who will build us up instead of tear us down is crucial in overcoming sin. Sin is a personal choice, yes, but if we have a band of brothers or sisters in Christ who will pray with us or for us, who will come to our aid when we struggle, and who will tell us what we need to hear, not what we want to hear, we will be set up to win this fight.

Find an accountability partner or group that will walk through this battle with you. All Christians should have someone they can talk to, but too often, it is a struggle to find someone. The truth is that it is even harder to find someone if you do not ask! James 5:16 commanded Christians to "confess your sins to each other." There is power in speaking a confession of our sin and having a brother or sister that we can turn to when we start down that path again.

Sin does not relent. If we win a battle, the war is still not over. Ephesians 6 tells us to put on the full armor of God. These components equip us as Christians to be ready for battle because we are in a battle. Christians who refuse to acknowledge the battle or incorrectly state that "God has already won" as a way of saying there's no more battles to face will find themselves as a target for Satan. Yes, God has ultimately won victory over sin through Jesus's death on the cross, but there's still work to be done, battles to be waged, ground to be taken, and chains to be broken until Jesus returns.

CHAPTER 4 REFLECTION AND DISCUSSION QUESTIONS

1. Why is sin still a problem for us as Christians? How do you personally measure your success in handling sin?

2. Why do so many Christians worry about the sins of others more so than their own? When is a time you have you found yourself guilty of this?

3. What does freedom as Christians really mean? How can Christians misuse their freedom in Christ?

4. What parallels do you see in the rules parents give children versus the rules that God gives us?

5. How does it feel to be stuck in the "sin cycle"? Reflect on a personal victory in this area and what made it possible?

6. Why is it hard to give others advice on their personal struggles with sin? What is important to remember when giving advice to others?

7. If you have an accountability partner, how has it benefitted you? If you do not have one, who do you think you could ask to hold you accountable?

CHAPTER 5:
DISCERNMENT WITH TIME

When you are young, time seems never ending; you want it to speed up because you can't wait to get older. When you are older, you want time to slow down because you know our time here on Earth is limited. William Penn said:

> *"There is nothing of which we are apt to be so lavish as of Time, and about which we ought to be more solicitous; since without it we can do nothing in this World. Time is what we want most, but what, alas! we use worst; and for which God will certainly most strictly reckon with us, when Time shall be no more."*[1]

Consider this poem by Henry Twells called "Times Places":

> *When as a child I laughed and wept,*
> *Time crept.*
> *When as a youth I waxed more bold,*
> *Time strolled.*
> *When I became a full grown man,*
> *Time RAN.*
> *When older still I daily grew,*
> *Time FLEW.*
> *Soon I shall find, in passing on,*
> *Time gone.*[2]

KAIROS AND CHRONOS

To understand the importance of having discernment with our time, I want to take a look at time from God's perspective and ways that the Bible conveys how God moves and shows His sovereignty over His creation.

Time is a creation of God; the entire universe was formed at God's command (Heb. 11:3). Understanding how God functions in His creation of time gives us some insight into the nature of God. There are two Greek words for time, *kairos* and *chronos*, but they imply different things. *Chronos* refers to minutes and seconds; it refers to time as a measurable duration. *Kairos* refers to time as an appointed time, a due season, or a specific point in time, a "strike point" moment.

We live our lives in the *chronos* mindset; we monitor the year by the month and day it is. We measure how long we have until a vacation or a birthday. We monitor our day by what hour we come home from work or when we go to bed. But even in our *chronos* lives, we can think of certain *kairos* or strike point moments that happened over the course of our lives that defined who we are, that changed a course of action, or that brought tremendous stress.

God works within the two forms of time. The Israelites were in slavery during *chronos* time, awaiting their freedom. In a *kairos* moment, God sends Moses who starts a chain of plagues and miracles and crosses the Red Sea into freedom.

Jesus had many *kairos* moments during the course of His *chronos* ministry. When Jesus intervened in any of His miracles, they were *kairos* moments. He powerfully changed the course of someone's *chronos* timeline during those miracles. Jesus's *chronos* ministry ended in a *kairos* moment with His words on the cross, "It is finished." Romans 5:6 says, "At just the right time [*kairos*] when we were still powerless, Christ died for the ungodly." Again, with Jesus's resurrection, this was a *kairos* moment where He overcame sin and death for everyone.

We wait now in the *chronos*, awaiting the day when Jesus returns in a *kairos* moment. He will victoriously proclaim again that "it is finished" (Rev. 21:6).

Paul tells us in Ephesians to take advantage of the time (*kairos*) because the days are evil. We need to be aware of the strike point moments in our lives where we can use discernment and take advantage of the time. This could be a moment in our day when someone needs us to show him love. This could be a stranger we meet that we feel called to witness to. This can also be a moment during the craziness of the day that we set aside for prayer.

We also need to have discernment in the chronos time of our lives. We have one life to live, and the decisions we make about the course of actions should align with the plans and direction in which God is leading us. Some of these decisions are who we marry, where we live, what career we choose, where we go to school, etc.

It's important to wait on God's timing. God is not slow as we count slowness (2 Pet. 3:9). Sometimes, we do not see the big picture over the course of *chronos* history. Sometimes, it is up to us to take advantage of each *kairos* moment we are given and not let time slip away from us where we leave behind a wasted life.

Some of what happens to us is the result of living in a sinful world. Living in the *chronos* timeframe, things will happen to us and around us as a result of the sin process that will not fully be restored until the final kairos moment of redemption of this fallen world, a New Heaven and a New Earth where there will be no more death or sorrow or crying or pain (Rev. 21:4).

TIME IS NOT ON YOUR SIDE

One year between birthdays seems like an eternity when you are young. When you get older, it feels like you blink and a decade has passed. We need to consider time as a limited resource, and because of that, we are not guaranteed tomorrow. Our day is filled with making one choice after another. Many choices we make subliminally. It's amazing how I can wake up for work, get ready, and drive to work without really making much of a cognizant effort because it is something I am used to doing out of habit.

We fall into the trap in our lives of establishing routines, for good or bad, without questioning "why do we do what we do?" I'm not saying that routines are bad. They can help keep our sanity, but they need to be evaluated and compared with our priorities and goals. If you *say* that you want to make more time for your kids but do not put into *action* a realistic way of accomplishing that, you cannot be upset when it doesn't happen. The same applies if you *say* that you want to exercise and eat healthy. If you do not put into *action* a new eating and exercise regimen, you will continue to be stuck in old habits.

My mom always told me that we "make time for what's important to us." I always believed this simple phrase, but the older I get, the more it makes sense. When we say that there are things we do not have time for, it is never a matter of not actually having the minutes or hours, but it means we made other things more of a priority! Knowing that we do not have unlimited time, it is *all* about a matter of *priority.*

A term I learned in business school is "opportunity cost." It basically refers to the value of something you give up in order to choose something else. Every choice we make has an opportunity cost. Some have low impact. For example, if I go to the movies tonight, I am not at home finishing a book I wanted to read. Others have high impact such as, if I take this job that pays more, I have to move my family across the country and we will not be near our friends and family.

We need to weigh our choices in consideration of the opportunity costs associated with them. Being presented with opportunities can be a great chance to show love, to resolve a broken relationship, to bring healing to a hurt, to speak truth to someone that needs to hear it, to impact a community, and to tell others about Jesus. Think about what the consequences are when I choose to not go to church, to not volunteer, to not read my Bible, to not pray.

Sometimes, the impact of our choices is not evident immediately. Over time, the impact of not praying, for example, could lead to a lack of closeness with God, a lack of peace, being more prone to anger, or a feeling of hopelessness. The impact of not making quality time with your kids might not reveal consequences until they are older when you have lost a deep connection with them and they refuse to submit to your authority as a parent.

Most people's Monday through Friday routines looks familiar each day. If you need to write out your routines and the time it takes for each activity, it may help you see that you are missing out on key priorities. Decide what priorities are important to you and make sure they fit within your schedule!

PRIORITIZE

How would you rank these things on your priority scale (if they apply)? Family, Work, God, Hobbies, Children, Church, and Spouse.

If God is not number one on your list, your list is wrong, bottom line. This does not mean that work and family are not important. Quite the contrary, only by God being the number one priority in your life are you able to fully and properly devote yourself to all the other things on the list. A husband or father filled with the Holy Spirit and in communion with God throughout the day is able to be the man he is called to be for his family and lead them properly.

We are called the Bridegroom of Christ in the Bible. If you are married, how did you act when you were dating, awaiting the day you would be married? For me, I know I wanted to be around my soon-to-be wife at all times; she was and is my best friend. I show her my love by the time I spend with her, making her an important part of my day as often as possible. The same should be said for our relationship with Jesus. If we struggle to put together five minutes a day to read His Word and pray, we are showing Him that He is not a priority for us regardless of what we say, how aggressively we defend the faith, or how loudly we sing a worship song.

Luke 10:38-42 is a short but powerful story of Mary and Martha. Mary and Martha invites Jesus into their home, but they each have two very different ways of spending their time with Him. Martha is worried about the tasks around the house; she is probably cleaning, cooking, and tidying up. Mary, however, uses the time with Jesus to sit at His feet and listen to Him.

Martha, overly frustrated by her sister, gives Jesus a command, which is bold in and of itself. Martha asks Jesus if He cares that Mary has left all the work to her. Keep in mind she is talking to the most caring person that ever lived Who came to Earth to die for her sins. Here Martha is only concerned about the *works* and not the *relationship* with Jesus! Jesus lovingly calms her by saying, "Martha, Martha, thou art careful and troubled about many things: But one thing is needful: and Mary hath chosen that good part, which shall not be taken away from her (Luke 10:41-42 KJV).

Both of the women in this example loved Jesus, both were "Christians," but like today, many Christians place the wrong emphasis on how they build a relationship with Jesus. Many Christians are involved in tasks and deeds to prepare for Jesus's Kingdom, yet He is already here living in their hearts. If we are too involved in tasks *for* Jesus without getting to *know* Jesus, we miss the "good part" that Jesus told Martha about. We have to make time for God each day, and only then will we find the purpose and fulfillment in any action we make in Jesus's name. Without being plugged in to the source of living water, all our actions and activities will lead to spiritual thirst.

Our actions definitely have a purpose and place for God's Kingdom here on Earth, but they must be preceded by a relationship with our King first!

FEELINGS CANNOT BE TRUSTED

Too often, we rely on our feelings to prioritize our time and decisions. If we don't "feel" like exercising, we sit on the couch. If we don't "feel" like eating right, we grab fast food. If we don't "feel" like spending time with our children, we go see a movie. Feelings are terrible catalysts for discernment. We need to follow through on what we *know* is right instead of listening to our feelings. Don't let your feelings control your faith.

How often have you gone to school or work despite "feeling" like it? Probably most days.

Proverbs 16:3 tells us to "commit to the Lord whatever you do, and he will establish your plans." We need to incorporate routines into our life that help us achieve our goals. If you want to get fit, you must spend X number of hours working out. If you want to get a degree, you must commit years of dedication to school.

The same goes with having a relationship with Jesus. If we *say* that we want one, we *have* to commit to following the steps to get there. This starts with spending time reading the Bible and praying daily. How long depends on you, but if you start small and get comfortable with that, it can grow in time. However, you cannot attempt this for five minutes a day, get distracted while you are "spending time with God," and then check off the task like everything else you do during the day to get spiritual brownie points. The worst for me is spending time reading *right* before bed. I'm already half asleep, and then, if I try to actively be involved with what I am reading and listen to the Holy Spirit, it usually ends with me asleep or forgetting what I just read.

Find what works for you and your routines. Ideally, if you can find time to set apart from the noise around you where you can meditate on the Bible, then make it happen. Many times, we think that time with God *has* to look a certain way. However, consider that the Bible tells us to "pray without ceasing" (1 Thess. 5:17). We can take time during our day to pray, stop, and pray again later.

I text my wife many times throughout the day when I am not with her; usually, it is to tell her I love her, communicate my frustrations, ask what is going on later, let her know when I am coming home, and vice versa. Prayer should be a constant communication with our Heavenly Father who wants to us to express our love, joys, fears, and doubts to Him daily.

By using discernment with our time, we can cognitively decide how we need to spend it. There are plenty of times when I just need to relax and watch something mind-numbing after a hard day's work. In the meantime, I need to be aware of what I am giving up when doing this. Like anything, balance is important when we use our time. There's absolutely nothing wrong with lounging around, giving time to a hobby, watching a movie, or hanging out with friends. If your entire day every day is spent doing these things while neglecting important things like work, family, prayer, church, etc., then there's a serious problem.

It's okay to stop and smell the roses as long as you aren't neglecting the rest of the garden!

There are obviously tools available to help you plan your day; I'm not talking about those here. What I want to make sure is clear from this chapter is that we need to use spiritually-led discernment with our time, to make the best use of the time we are given. What is your role right now in furthering God's Kingdom here on Earth until He returns? Are we fulfilling the Great Commission, or are we too self-absorbed to care for those hurting around us that need Jesus? If someone just *looked* at your schedule each day, could they tell you were a Christian?

CHAPTER 5 REFLECTION AND DISCUSSION QUESTIONS

1. How has your view of time changed with each new stage of your life?

2. Give specific examples of how God has moved in the *kairos* (strikepoint) and *chronos* (over time) in your life.

3. Why does God's timing not make sense to us as humans? Give an example of when you felt this way.

4. Give an example of an opportunity cost (something you gave up in order to favor something else) based on a decision you made. In hindsight, was this the right decision, why or why not?

5. What are your priorities, and how are these reflected in the ways you spend your time?

6. Why are feelings said to be a poor master? How have your feelings gotten you in trouble in the past?

7. What are you convicted about in regard to having discernment with your time after reading this chapter?

CHAPTER 6:
DISCERNMENT WITH WORDS

How many words does the average person speak in a day? While there are factors such as age, culture, and work environment at play, one study found that the average person speaks around 16,000 words a day![1] With these thousands of words coming out of our mouths daily, it would be safe to say that discernment with our words is very important!

We've all probably heard this phrase as kids: "Sticks and stones may break my bones, but words will never hurt me." When we get older, we realize that words do indeed hurt. Words hurt especially when they come from someone we care about. Negative words from someone we respect cut deep to our core. Unfortunately, those who know us best seem to know what to say in a time of anger to really make an impact on our emotions. We may try to act tough and pretend that negative words do not affect us, but as humans, we are driven by the positive or negative feedback from those around us.

We know what it is like to receive positive verbal feedback. There is a sense of accomplishment when you hear from a teacher or boss that you did a good job. You cannot help but feel valued and loved when a spouse or child tells you how much you mean to him or her. Even if we already know we are loved, hearing it again expressed in words confirms those feelings and squashes any doubt.

We have more power in our words than we give ourselves credit for. My Dad would always tell me when I was growing up to "think before you speak." This is where discernment comes into play. We have to analyze what we are going to say, determine whether or not the words coming out of our mouths are going to build someone up or tear them down, and ask ourselves if we will regret saying them. We then can fall back on the other popular saying of "if you don't have something nice to say, don't say anything at all." Many times, we speak out of strong emotions like anger, fear, or pride. Using discernment allows us to think outside of those emotions; if we would not be proud of saying something later on after the emotions have subsided, we should show restraint.

It's important to note that, while our words are powerful enough to affect those around us, they do *not* have power in and of themselves. Words are not filled with a "secret power" like New Age movements will tell you. You cannot speak into the universe that you want to win the lottery, for example, and watch the stars align for you. We will continue by discussing what the Bible has to say about our words and how we can use discernment with others we come into contact with.

THE POWER OF THE TONGUE

The Bible has a lot to say about the tongue and the power of our words. Proverbs 18:21 says, "The tongue has the power of life and death, and those who love it will eat its fruit."

James Chapter 3:1-12 has some serious warnings about the power of the tongue and its effects on those around us. James likens the tongue, something so small that affects something much larger, to a ship's rudder in its ability to direct and steer and to the way a horse's bit controls the direction of the horse (v. 3-4). Neither a rudder nor a bit has control on its own just like a tongue has no power; it is just a chunk of muscular tissue! The control of our tongue all depends on the person *operating* it just as a captain has full control of the ship or a rider control of the horse through the leverage of something so small.

More than likely, James was speaking to a body of believers where many of them wanted to teach and preach. He warns them in verse 1 of chapter 3 that "not many of you should act as teachers, my brothers, because you know that we who teach will be judged more strictly." They could have been so impressed with the authority and prestige of the position that they forgot about the responsibility and accountability that comes with such a position.

Teachers and preachers today who use their words to spread the gospel need to be aware of what they are saying and if it is spoken in alignment with the truth of the Bible and God's Word. The damage done by a teacher who does not spread God's Word is severe; furthermore, a teacher who does not practice what he preaches is guilty of hypocrisy.

The same warning applies to those who may not preach the Word of God directly but, at the same time, realize that their life is an example to others through words and actions. Posters during World War II cautioned the population that "LOOSE LIPS SINK SHIPS." This was an attempt to curb the propaganda that could lead to dissention or lower morale at a fragile time during the war as well as keep trade secrets from falling into enemy hands. The truth is that loose lips also wreck lives. A person who makes a careless statement may find himself in either a verbal or physical fight. The tongue has forced the rest of your body to defend itself.

James also likens the tongue to a fire which can destroy a forest and how the tongue is full of poison and cannot be tamed like an animal (v. 3:5-8).

A fire usually starts small and ends up consuming all around it when it is not controlled. A fire reportedly started in the O'Leary barn in Chicago at 8:30 P.M.,

October 8, 1871. And because that fire spread, over 100,000 people were left homeless, 17,500 buildings were destroyed, and 300 people died. It cost the city over $400 million.[2]

As fire spreads and receives more fuel, the more destructive it is. The words we speak have the power to destroy. Proverbs 26:20 says, "Without wood a fire dies out; without a gossip a quarrel dies down." A gossip is referred to in the Bible as anyone who cannot control his or her words. I feel Christians might hear the word gossip and often think of "that one church lady" who struggles with gossip while dismissing any application to them. We need to resist the urge to feed the fire of rumors and lies, especially in the Body of Christ. We need to go to the person we have a conflict with and try to resolve it in love and grace. If a resolution is not possible, it stops there; it does not need to make the headlines of the "local Christian news network."

We can be guilty of fueling this fire just by simply listening to gossip and negative talk. We justify ourselves by saying "I'm not the one saying it" or "I'm just being a good friend by listening," but we are just as guilty. We can be a friend without perpetuating the negative flow of content coming from our friend's mouth. We can either remove ourselves from a situation where gossip occurs or use our words to diffuse the situation.

The term "fight fire with fire" comes from the tactic used by firefighters to start a fire with a controlled burn that will consume resources before the bigger fire arrives. In the same way, we need to use our positive words of truth to combat lies and negative words that we encounter from others, we should not add to the fuel that will sustain this negativity.

James finally likens the tongue to a spring of water and a tree bearing fruit (v. 9-12). Fresh water coming from a spring can produce life in the sustainability of the water and its ability to provide for those who come to the source. Water, like our words, can give life and cleanse.

Just as a water source cannot provide fresh and saltwater, so our words lose their ability to delight and enrich those around us when we mix in love and hate. We lose our witness as Christians when we bless the Lord in worship and go and curse His creation made in His image! Saint Francis of Assisi has been commonly credited with saying, "Preach the gospel, and if necessary, use words."[3] Our words can get in our way, and if we cannot control them, it is best to have discernment about what we are saying and if it is the right timing to actually say it.

When in doubt of what to say, simply listen. When we listen to those hurting around us and show a genuine interest in what others have to say, we show empathy and that we care about them as people without always needing to get involved with our opinions.

The true "heart" of the matter is shown to us in Matthew 12:34, "For the mouth speaks what the heart is full of." When Jesus controls our heart, our lips are controlled as a result.

WORDS WITH OUR SPOUSES

Why is it that there is often conflict with the person that we love the most, our spouses? We are called to unity with our spouses, and our words are often the biggest catalyst for strife in a marriage. Why? Because we know exactly how to hurt our spouses. We know them better than anyone, and if we do not use discernment about what we are saying, we may choose the words that cut like a sword into their very soul when we let emotions take control.

The goal is not to eliminate conflict in marriage. In fact, conflict can be a good thing; it resolves mixed opinions, it creates a unified approach to a situation, and it determines the path that should be taken before more confusion happens. Negative conflict is one that seeks to destroy feelings, to not seek a resolution, and that isn't based on the foundation of love.

Our words to our spouses should build them up; we should use our words to pray, to encourage them, and remind them of our love. Unfortunately, I feel prayer together is often neglected in a Christian marriage. Prayer together makes you vulnerable, it can be intimidating, and it can feel awkward if you don't have the "right words to say." But prayer can also be powerful, adding a new connection on a spiritual level that allows for increased intimacy (not just sexual!).

My wife, Jamie, and I would lead marriage groups at church, and one exercise we always did during the course was having couples pray together at the end of a session, taking turns while facing each other, holding each other's hands. The feedback we received was always positive, usually something along the lines of "that was great; we need to do more of that" or "we rarely ever pray together, and now, I know that is an area we are lacking in together."

One couple in particular had been married for five years and had never prayed for each other out loud before. This seems like a very simple act, but it is easy to neglect. Like anything, the more you practice something, the easier it is to do. I would encourage you to start praying with your spouse, however awkward it is at first; God will use that to bless you both and grow your relationship together.

Wives are called to submit to their husbands (Eph. 5:22), but right after that verse, men are given a high standard to follow.

> *Husbands, love your wives, just as Christ loved the church and gave himself up for her to make her holy, cleansing her by the washing with water through the word, and to present her to himself as a radiant church, without stain or wrinkle or any other blemish, but holy and blameless (Eph. 5:25-27).*

Neither spouse is greater than the other; both are called to die to self for the benefit of the marriage. If we die to self, we die to our wants. If we die to our wants, we do not always say what we "want" to say but, sometimes, what needs to be said. This may mean something as simple as saying you will go to a restaurant you do not like (without letting it be known that you don't want to go). It could mean giving of your time to listen to your mate speak about her day, lifting her up in encouragement during a rough day with words of affirmation and comforting her with all the reasons she means so much to you.

Francis Chan has provided some great insight into his own marriage and how they handle arguments and conflict in the following interview:

> *Okay. Yes. Lisa and I argue. Honestly, we don't argue that much because we realize we don't have time for this. We are on a mission. She describes it like there is a TV show called The Amazing Race where couples are racing to get to this finish line and they are competing with other couples, but you see certain ones fight and they start losing ground and they argue with each other and lose the race. And we look at our lives very much like that, like there are things for us to do and we are here to seek His kingdom. We are here to make disciples. And if we spend our time just fighting with each other, it is going to keep us from His mission, and so one of the ways we can fight is always realizing, okay, divorce isn't an option and also we don't have a lot of time to argue about petty things because we are*

dealing with eternal things, and so we keep that in our minds.

The goal is becoming like Jesus. And the goal is not winning an argument. It is pleasing Christ, becoming like Christ, and most of the time, the person who "wins the argument" is usually the one who acts least like Jesus. And so we keep that in mind that God opposes the proud. And so I could win this argument in a sense, but if I do it in arrogance, now, suddenly, I have got God opposing me. So what did I win? I am a loser at that point, so it is like: Okay, humble myself.

Treat her like God's daughter and remember that we have got things to do for the Kingdom. We cannot waste our time arguing about things that are not eternal. So let me humble myself. If it is not a big deal, then just let it go. Let her have her way. There is more important things to focus on.[4]

When we are at odds with our spouses, regardless of the reasons, we are losing ground in the fight for our family. The enemy gains a foothold when there is unresolved strife or negative words. A good rule is, when you feel like saying something hurtful to your spouse, give him or her a hug instead. An action as small and seemingly insignificant as a hug can really help diffuse a negative situation. It only takes one person, sometimes, to step out of the emotions and feelings being displayed and help both parties realize the bigger picture...that they love each other greatly despite the current frustrations.

Most of the conflict with our spouses comes when both sides are not committed to God with their words. If God has not gotten a hold of the heart of your spouse *yet*, pray. Live the example set in Proverbs 15:1, "A gentle answer turns away wrath, but a harsh word stirs up anger." When both sides are functioning with discernment in their words for the benefit of the marriage, it can be a beautiful thing for God's glory.

WORDS WITH OUR CHILDREN

We need discernment when speaking with our children. Words have the power to make them feel encouraged, like they can do anything, or it can cripple them with feelings of self-doubt and frustration. Unfortunately, parents, many times, allow their children to set the tone for the conversation in their household. If a child escalates in frustration, it is very hard to not respond likewise. The result of this can be a shouting match with words spewing out that both parties will regret later.

The Bible tells fathers, "Don't' exasperate your children by coming down hard on them. Take them by the hand and lead them in the way of the Master" (Eph. 6:4, MSG). This is not an instruction against discipline; it is about understanding your children's hearts and leading them. It is true for both parents, but I believe it is directed at fathers because we can be the hardest on our children, wanting the best for them but many times alienating them in the process. This is not to say that it cannot happen with mothers as well, but they tend to add the nurturing component of parenting that may be harder for a father to show.

Parents expecting perfection can lead their children to the point of mental and emotional breakdown. I personally have to remember this when my children make mistakes at home, school, or sporting events. I try to remember to use learning moments and let them be a part of the solution instead of displaying frustrations or spouting off an explanation of what they did wrong.

As parents, we need to understand that our words have power as the authority in our children's lives. A rule of thumb is that it can take ten positive statements to undo one negative one. If we figuratively speak death to our children in terms of tearing them down, they will tend to hold on to that as truth even if we apologize later or take them out for ice cream.

What exactly does life and death in our words with our children look like? It can be explained as follows: "Life speaks to a child's personhood, positive performance, and potential. Death constantly points out a child's failure, mistakes, and misguided thoughts, feelings, and attitudes. You are not your child's accuser, judge, or prosecuting attorney. You are your child's teacher, supporter, encourager, and godly parent."[5]

NOW I LAY ME DOWN TO SLEEP

Do you pray with your children? I'm not talking about on the side of the bed at bedtime, which is fine and well. We need to pray with our children and speak blessings over them. We need to call out the strengths in them, that they will use them for God and His Kingdom. We need to let them know that God has a purpose and plan for them.

Blessing your children has a foundational base in the Bible. Jacob coveted Isaac's blessing (Gen. 27:19), Joseph blessed his sons before he died (Gen. 48:20), Laban blessed his grandchildren and daughters (Gen. 31:55), Joshua blessed Caleb (Josh. 14:13), Saul blessed David as "his son" (1 Sam. 26:25), and Jesus took children into His arms and blessed them (Mark 10:16).

The Aaronic priestly blessing is described in Numbers 6:24-26. Aaron, as High Priest, and his sons were commanded to bless the Israelites saying, "The Lord bless you and keep you; the Lord make his face to shine on you and be gracious to you; the Lord turn his face toward you and give you peace." This priestly blessing was not just used for the Israelites at the time but has been used for generations to bless children and is a model for us today.

The word "bless" is translated from barak (H1288 in Strong's dictionary). It means "to bless, kneel, salute, or greet."[6] In the Old Testament, it means "to endue with power for success, prosperity, fecundity, longevity, etc."[7]

Barak can also mean to praise or adore. But why would my God praise or *barak* me as in "the Lord bless you and keep you?" The creation is not worthy of its Creator's praise. Jesus came as the suffering servant, taking the weight of our sins on His back as He went to Calvary. God does not physically kneel down before us, but in a way, Jesus knelt down to our level like a parent kneeling before his children to come to their eye level. We are blessed by God who sent His only son to come live and die as a human, who took away the condemnation and eternal punishment that our sin deserved.

When we "bless" our children with our words, we are figuratively kneeling before them, coming to their level, and giving of our time and honor, showing them with our words and actions that they mean the world to us.

Discipline undeniably has its place in parenting. Discipline, like anything, requires balance. If you only speak in negative words to your children in response for what they do and if these words are regrettably in anger, you have the potential for a child who will either lack confidence in himself or will constantly struggle to gain either parent's favor.

Our words have the power to tear down and build up. Our children need the confidence in themselves that only the words of their parents can give them. Parents need to recognize the many ways children are gifted, creative, and sensitive to God. Speaking a blessing over your children in addition to daily encouragement is a focused way of ensuring your children feel the love and approval of their parents and their God.

WORDS IN THE BODY OF CHRIST

Have you heard the following interaction in your church?

Person A: "How's it going, brother?"

Person B: "I'm blessed. God is good."

Person A: "All the time! Praise God!"

What is wrong with this? Well, nothing... there's just no depth to it. If we are to use discernment in our words among our brothers and sisters in Christ, shouldn't we aspire to something more encouraging and fulfilling with the time we have with each other?

Here are some Bible verses that direct us in how we are to act with one another:

- "Bear with each other and forgive one another if any of you has a grievance against someone" (Col. 3:13).
- "Carry each other's burdens, and in this way you will fulfill the law of Christ" (Gal. 6:2).
- "Confess your sins to each other and pray for each other so that you may be healed. The prayer of a righteous person is powerful and effective" (James 5:16).
- "As iron sharpens iron, so one person sharpens another" (Prov. 27:17).
- "'For where two or three gather in my name, there am I with them'" (Matt. 18:20).

• "Each of you should use whatever gift you have received to serve others, as faithful stewards of God's grace in its various forms" (1 Pet. 4:10).

The first step in this process is to establish a relationship with someone. Once we have that, we should focus on encouraging our brethren in their walk with God. We should pray for one another and be humble enough to ask for prayer as well. A Christian who puts up an impenetrable wall around him or herself cannot give or receive.

Christians who try to fight sin and struggle by themselves often find themselves overwhelmed by their opposition. We need people close to us that we can call on to pray with, to confess when we struggle, and to encourage us when we fall. The entire church does not need to know, but if we have a close "band of brothers" or sisters that we are accountable to, we have a greater chance of winning the battles when they come...and they *will* come.

I can speak to the following for the men in churches I have seen and myself because I am guilty. We are quick to be sarcastic and joke with one another. We are quick to talk about the latest movie that just came out. We are quick to complain about our jobs and family. However, we are slow to ask what God is doing in each other's lives or ask, "How can I pray for you today?" We are slow to speak encouragement into another person's life based on the gifts we see alive in him. We are slow to use our spiritual gifts to edify the body of believers as we are called to do (1 Cor. 14:26).

If the purpose of having discernment with our words with our brethren is to edify and not destroy, we need to consider how our words, or lack thereof, are being used to glorify God and build up Christians around us.

What effect would the following *example* dialogue have in the church today?

"John, I see you every week faithful in serving this church. I wanted to thank you but also call out those gifts in you, the heart you have for people, and encourage you to let God continue to use you in new and amazing ways. Lean on Jesus and let me know how I can pray for you. I am here for you."

The additional aspect to this is to let the Spirit guide you in "words of wisdom and knowledge" for people (1 Cor. 12:8). If you prepare your heart before Sunday or an interaction with someone, God may have His Spirit move in you to speak a word or blessing over someone that you could not have prepared ahead of time. Again, this does not need to happen with every conversation, but if we let God direct us, they should happen as the Spirit leads.

CHAPTER 6 REFLECTION AND DISCUSSION QUESTIONS

1. Give an example of a time when you did not have discernment with your words and it led to a negative or unintended consequence.

2. Why does the book of James give so many warnings against the misuse of the tongue? How can the tongue be used for both good and evil?

3. In what ways have you seen gossip permeate the Church? How have you participated in it within your own church?

4. In marriage, how can words both build up and destroy your spouse? Give examples.

5. How can your words as a parent be used to build up your children versus tearing them down?

6. How is prayer used in your walk with Jesus and your family? In what ways can it be improved upon?

7. How can words be used in the Body of Christ to strengthen others and build them up?

CHAPTER 7:
DISCERNMENT WITH FINANCES

Before I start writing about discernment with our finances, let me make a note on the fact that, like most topics in this book, it is impossible to try and comprehensively write on this topic in one chapter when there are a multitude of books out there about this. I will discuss some key points about finances in the perspective of the bigger conversation around discernment. If you want further information on how to budget and use your finances wisely, there is no better expert on this subject, in my opinion, than Dave Ramsey. Any of his books will provide you wisdom in this as they are biblically sound as well as practically savvy.

WHOSE MONEY IS IT?

It's easy to consider the money that I worked so hard for to be "my money," but it is important to understand that everything is the Lord's and we are simply in a managerial role of how to disperse the money we are given. Psalm 24:1 tells us that, "The Earth is the Lord's and everything in it, the world, and all who live in it." The thought that God owns everything including our money can be a sobering one; it forces us to keep an eternal perspective on our decision-making. We are simply stewards, or servants, with what we are entrusted.

When children are small, they have an immense possession over toys and things that are given to them. If you try to take one away, you might get a response of "That's mine!" We know, however, that the children spent no money on the toy; their loving parent gave it to them. When my daughter was 3 years old, she yelled at her brother for looking out *her* window in the car. She obviously did not own the car. My son also told his sister one time to get out of *his* room. He did not own the house. When we tell God to "get out of our finances," either by words or actions, we make the same mistake of incorrectly identifying ownership of said finances.

Jesus gave the example of the faithful steward in Luke 12:42-48. Jesus finishes the parable by saying, "'From everyone who has been given much, much will be demanded; and from the one who has been entrusted with much, much more will be asked'" (v. 48). The blessings we have, the knowledge we acquire, and the monetary gains we make should all be used to glorify God while we fill our time on Earth. That does not mean that we should not buy fun things we can afford as long as we keep in mind that we are stewards to God for our finances.

TWO MASTERS

The problems with money arise when we have mixed loyalty. We try to serve two masters. Jesus warns about this in Matthew 6:24.

> *"'No one can serve two masters. Either you will hate the one and love the other, or you will be devoted to the one and despise the other. You cannot serve both God and money.'"*

With Jesus as our focus, we will be less likely to chase the possessions. Real wealth and happiness are about our attitudes and knowing who we serve, not dollars in a bank account. If you study lottery winners and celebrities, you will find some of the saddest people who have a lack of contentment. After the glitter and glamour fades, which seems exciting at first, there is little fulfillment in worldly endeavors.

John D. Rockefeller, a Christian millionaire, said, "I have made many millions, but they have brought me no happiness. I would barter them all for the days I sat on an office stool in Cleveland and counted myself rich on three dollars a week."[1]

W. H. Vanderbilt said, "The care of 200 million dollars is too great a load for any brain or back to bear. It is enough to kill anyone. There is no pleasure in it."[1]

John Jacob Astor left five million dollars after he died but had been struggling with indigestion and melancholy. He said, "I am the most miserable man on earth."[1]

Henry Ford, the automobile king, said, "Work is the only pleasure. It is only work that keeps me alive and makes life worth living. I was happier when doing a mechanic's job."[1]

Andrew Carnegie, the multi-millionaire, said, "Millionaires seldom smile."[1]

NEEDS VS. WANTS

In order to have discernment in our finances, we need to distinguish between needs and wants. We've all heard or been a part of the receiving end of the child who screams in the store, "I NEED THAT TOY!" As parents, it's easy to tell your child that she does not need it even though it's less easy to calm her down about it. As adults, we face the same temptation of seeing a new flashy item and inwardly saying that we need it without the fanfare of a tantrum...hopefully. Is it bad to buy items that we don't need?

The needs we have in life are simple: food, water, shelter. There are some needs that are not as primitive in nature such as needing transportation to get to the job that provides food on the table and needing clothes for said job. Just because we need to eat, does that mean that we need to have Filet Mignon every night? Of course not. What is important in considering needs vs. wants is our budget. We should have a budget for items that we want to buy, and if we cannot afford them, we shouldn't buy them. If money is tight and your kids need clothes, your house needs repairs, and your wife has withheld her wants for the good of the family, then it would be pretty clear that you do *not* need to buy that boat you have been eyeing...

There are often more important things to focus on that money cannot buy. Consider the poem:

Money will buy:

A bed, but not sleep.
Books, but not brains.
Food, but not appetite.
A house, but not a home.
Medicine, but not health.
Amusement, but not happiness.
Finery, but not beauty.
A crucifix, but not a Savior.[2]

Money and worry tend to go hand in hand. It is usually the number one cause for divorce among Christian and non-Christian marriages. Jesus, however, tells us not to worry about "'what you will eat or drink; or about your body, what you will wear. Is not life more than food, and the body more than clothes?'" (Matt. 6:25). Worrying in general, but especially about finances, keeps us focused on things that do not really matter. We are also told by Jesus to store up treasures in heaven because "'where your treasure is, there your heart will be also'" (Matt. 6:21). If our hearts are in the wealth we can achieve, the pursuit of money, and the accumulation of "toys," we will not have the time to focus on what our call is as Christians, to know Him and make Him known.

GIVING BACK TO GOD

It's an easier pill to swallow for some Christian to tell them to budget and be good stewards of their finances, but when you mention tithing, a figurative wall gets built and they may hold on more tightly to "their" money. We've already discussed how our money, blessings, and even our lives are not our own. Why is tithing such a problem for some? Some may believe the lie when they see the pastor's car and think, "The church is doing okay; they don't need my money." Now you should have discernment about *where* you give your tithe but not *if* you give your tithe. Your tithe should go where you are being spiritually fed.

Some may not understand the concepts laid out in the Bible for tithing. Also, some may be turned away by prosperity preaching when they gave in the past and did not get the "prosperity" that was promised to them by false evangelists. Whatever the reason, it is important to look to the Bible and have discernment about what we are called to do.

The concept of tithing is found all throughout the Bible. The Israelites were instructed to tithe the best of their crops and animals to the Lord in the amount of ten percent (Deut. 14:22). When presenting offerings, they were frequently commanded to give animals "without defect" (Levi. 3:1). These instructions are an example to us today that we give back to God as recognition of His sovereignty and who is in control of everything. The Israelites gave from the "firstfruits" of their crops and income as a sign of importance to God (Prov. 3:9-10). They did not scrape together some loose change to throw in the offering plate after all their bills and toys were paid for.

God also chastised the Israelites in Malachi 3 for withholding their tithe from Him. God speaks to Israel, "'Will a mere mortal rob God? Yet you rob me. But you ask, "How are we robbing you?" In tithes and offerings'" (v. 8). God follows this up with a promise of blessing. "'Bring the whole tithe into the storehouse... test me in this and see if I will not throw open the floodgates of heaven and pour out so much blessing that there will not be room enough to store it'" (v. 10).

God can do more with our 90 percent than we can do with our 100 percent. If we are faithful in tithing, the Bible promises blessing; however, this is not always a monetary blessing. We do not give to get. If anyone tells you that, if you give X amount, God will bless you 10x that amount or something to that effect, he is a false teacher. We need to give generously and with abundance, for God "loves a cheerful giver" (2 Cor. 9:7).

Our discernment as Christians is important when giving of our tithe. We need to make sure we are giving to the right person or church. I believe a church should be wise with its money as well and give out at least ten percent of all money coming into the mission field. If a church is not being prudent with its money, it is doing a disservice to its parishioners and to God. We need to use discernment with our money by budgeting and making sure that tithes are not an "optional" line item that we may or may not fulfill depending on the month. The ten percent is a changing amount depending on income. As income decreases, tithe can, too, but as income increases, so should the tithe!

As income increases, usually the standard of living does as well. It's easy to want to celebrate a new higher-paying job with a new house, car, or vacation, but discernment is needed to know if this is a wise choice for you and your family. As the standard of living you create for yourself increases, a feeling that you *never have enough money* is also created even though most of the world lives off of a fraction of what the average American makes. Being wise stewards as Christians, maybe the standard of living does not *have* to increase just because our income does. This allows more of a buffer to be generous and not stress out about bills.

Jesus pointed out the offering of the poor widow in Mark 12, telling the disciples that she "'put more into the treasury than all the others. They all gave out of their wealth; but she, out of her poverty, put in everything-all she had to live on'" (v. 43-44). This brings up the need to use discernment in our *motivations* with giving. If we curse under our breath as we give because "our spouses are making us," for example, we are missing the entire point. Our love for God should overflow in us to the point that we gladly give in abundance to the needs of the church, to the needs of our neighbors in our community and abroad.

COVETOUSNESS

I believe a lot of the problem with our discernment with our finances comes from covetousness. Not coveting is one of the Ten Commandments given from God to Moses (Ex. 20:17). Jesus expanded upon this in Matthew 6 when He commanded, "'Do not store up for yourselves treasures on earth'" (v. 19). Preceding that statement, Jesus said, "'The eye is the lamp of the body. If your eyes are healthy, your whole body will be full of light. But if your eyes are unhealthy, your whole body will be full of darkness'" (v. 22-23). Jesus made a connection between what we treasure on Earth and what we see. For what we see and dwell on can either provide goodness or darkness to our soul. Jesus stated that "'no one can serve two masters. Either you will hate the one and love the other, or you will be devoted to the one and despite the other. You cannot serve both God and money'" (Matt. 6:24).

I have fallen in the trap before in letting my eyes control my budget. I see a new car, TV, or other electronic device, and I immediately *need* it. I obsess over it, research it, watch videos to see it in action, read reviews, and compare prices. My free time is consumed with the thought of owning this new item until I eventually *have* it. It's funny because, most of the time, once you have that new thing, you move on to the next even *bigger* thing! There is little to no actual fulfillment in owning *things;* the pleasure quickly fades.

Money makes a terrible master, but no one worships their actual currency. When people see and desire that which they cannot have or usually afford, it can lead to strife. Married couples that argue over finances are usually in lack of agreement over what to spend their money on. If one spouse is especially superfluous in his or her spending, it creates strife with the other partner who might be trying to budget. James specifically states this when he says, "You covet but you cannot get what you want, so you quarrel and fight" (4:2).

Technology does not make this battle against envy any easier. When we covet today, it is easier to see what someone else has and want it. Just by looking on social media, you see all the new technology, cars, relationships, vacations, children, families, friends, etc. that other people have, and it is very easy to compare everything with your current situation.

The act of wanting something else, whether or not we can afford it, is not coveting. We should want to better ourselves, to learn more, to achieve success in our jobs, to have a life we can be proud of and that honors the Lord. The problem comes when we obsess over the things we cannot have, when we feel jealousy because someone else has it, when we become discontent with the blessings we have, and when we make unwise financial decisions in order to have it.

The definition of coveting is "to desire inordinately, to place the object of desire before love and devotion to God."[3] Mankind strives for what is forbidden and covets what is denied. This has been a fight since the Garden of Eden when Adam and Eve coveted the *one* thing they could not have. These desires arise from our earthly nature which we are called to put to death (Col. 3:5). The battle with coveting is not a matter of *if* but *when;* timing matters when it comes to finances. We must keep our thoughts and desires in check with the blessings and God's goodness to us, not taking them for granted.

Charles Spurgeon eloquently described coveting as:

> *A snake that can enter at the smallest hole. It lurks in the grass where it is long, but it glides also where the pasture is bare. It may come in either in prosperity or in adversity, and it is needful to whisper in the ear of each believer, whether going up or down in the world.*[4]

Many Christians might know Philippians 4:13, "I can do all things through him who gives me strength." Immediately before this verse, Paul is talking about contentment. "For I have learned to be content whatever the circumstances" (v. 11). "I know what it is to be in need, and I know what it is to have plenty, I have learned the secret of being content in any and every situation" (v. 12). The secret is being able to rely on Jesus for strength (v. 13). Paul adapted his life based on circumstances, no matter in blessing or need; he relied on Jesus for his strength.

If we rely on ourselves or "things" to drive us, we will never find contentment. A part of having discernment with our finances is understanding our needs vs. our wants and, ultimately, letting God be in control of our money. We need to control our lust, longing, and desires for what we don't have, cannot obtain, or cannot afford. Our strength, hope, and true riches are found in Jesus, the author and finisher of our faith (Heb. 12:2).

CHAPTER 7 REFLECTION AND DISCUSSION QUESTIONS

1. How were you raised to think of money and finances, and how has this affected your adult life?

2. Have you read any material from a financial advisor (i.e. Dave Ramsey), and what wisdom have you used relating to finances?

3. Why is it sometimes hard to think of God as owning everything, including our finances?

4. How can you be a "faithful steward" like the one in the parable Jesus gave?

5. Name some needs you have versus wants you have. Why is it hard to sometimes separate the two out when it comes to spending money?

6. Why are we commanded to give our tithes and offerings? How can this be misconstrued among Christians?

7. How does coveting relate to not having discernment with your finances?

CHAPTER 8:
DISCERNMENT WITH
RELATIONSHIPS

Why do we need discernment in our relationships? Have you ever been in a bad one? If you have, like most of us, then you know the damage a negative or even abusive relationship can have on your mental, spiritual, emotional, and physical health. This chapter will take a look at how we can live godly lives and have godly relationships while we are single or married and with the friends we have.

We will not always make (or have not always made) the perfect decisions in our relationships, and that is okay. However, what if we made these decisions within the context of the Bible, if we balanced our feelings with logic, and if we were grounded in being led by the Holy Spirit in our decision-making process?

THE SINGLE LIFE

I remember when I was single, there was a lot of angst about if and when I was going to get married. It felt like a question that I needed answered immediately, and when I didn't get an answer, it caused more anxiety and some bad choices.

When you are young and single, marriage feels like the finish line; however, when you grow in age and maturity, you realize marriage is really just the *starting line* to a new phase of your life. If I were to counsel my younger self, I would advise that I focus on using my time wisely, growing in maturity and getting myself ready to be the man of God that I was called to be. Instead of seeking that person to "complete me," I would first try to understand that only God can complete my life. Without the knowledge of who I was in Christ as a single man, which, thankfully, I arrived at before I was married, I could have never fully given of myself to my wife.

It turns out my "downtime" in between relationships was more of a blessing than I realized at the time. It caused me to learn from mistakes, to learn how to be alone, and to grow into the man that my wife was looking for. Everybody brings baggage into a relationship; this baggage is a result of poor relationships, insecurities, childhood experiences, and personality traits. The goal while you are single is to minimize the baggage into a carry-on vs. a full-blown suitcase!

Paul counsels the church in Corinth about those who are unmarried. It seems that Paul himself was unmarried and advocated celibacy (1 Cor. 7:8). He reasoned that, if Jesus is coming again soon, one could devote himself full-time to ministry to spread the gospel. Paul conceded that it is not wrong to marry, though (1 Cor. 7:36). Indeed, being single is an option for many Christians, and it should not be looked down on as a worse option if it is something you have peace with the Lord about. Sometimes, people need to be single for "a season." Singleness allows you time to pursue other activities like work or school, it gives you freedom to dedicate all of yourself to a ministry for the Lord, and it gives you the time to heal after a traumatic event (e.g. death or divorce).

The goal of discernment when being single, if it is your goal to find a mate, is to find someone who will build you up in Christ, enrich your life, and be a fulfillment to your spirit. If you believe marriage is a bond that cannot be broken, and you should, then you should take the decision seriously and not settle for the options that are simply in front of you. You may be ordering a fast food burger when there is choice steak waiting for you. Then again, God may be putting a person in your path for a reason; it comes down to discernment and not desperation.

It's important for the single person to choose wisely. There are a lot of choices out there, good and bad. It can almost cause a crippling effect of not wanting to make the wrong choice because you may not choose your "soulmate." Let me just state that I believe the Christian concept of "soulmate" to be false in how it is often portrayed. It can create a misconception that God will magically place a person at our front doorstep with a sign on him or her that says "pick me" with a halo of light around his or her head. We place our "soulmates" on a pedestal even above God and look for perfection when, in reality, Jesus was the only perfect person.

Thinking about our "soulmates" as the perfect people can lead to discontentment and even divorce. When our partners sin, discourage us, anger us, or frustrate us, we may think, "Well, that person isn't my soulmate. I must have chosen poorly." It discourages us from even trying. I'm not implying that some people do not choose poorly. They absolutely do, and many times, in the case of infidelity, it is out of the victim's control.

Ultimately, it is our choice who we marry, and it *can* be influenced by God. Once that choice is made, we then choose whether we will love, honor, and cherish that person for the rest of our lives. Writer and podcast host Stacey Sumereau has a great quote on this topic: "More important than finding 'the one' is choosing to love the one you chose."[1]

Sometimes, love is more than a feeling; it is a conscious choice. Actually, feelings are quite inconsequential when it comes to marriage. What matters is honoring the commitment and the vows that each couple made to one another *despite* their feelings!

Now that I am married, my wife is my soulmate. I have no more choices to make in the matter other than loving her and being the husband she needs me to be.

When we make the decision as single adults to focus on God and wait on the right timing, we need to rely on Him for wisdom. We need to understand what we are bringing to a relationship and if it is beneficial to each of our future spouses. Growing in the knowledge and the goodness of Jesus will be an attractive fragrance to the right type of partner you are looking for. If you are involved in sin or sinful activities, more than likely, you will attract the wrong person like flies to manure. If we allow Jesus to be the fragrant odor in our lives, we can find fulfillment in the choice for a partner we made with help from the Holy Spirit.

BE THE CHURCH

This section on discernment in our friendships does not seek to inform you on how to "make friends." We learn this in grade school; we know what good and bad friends look like. For some people, finding friends comes easier than it does for others. Some people do not need friends in their lives, or so they say.

Discernment is an important part of forming friendships. It's important to know what defines a healthy or unhealthy friendship with Christian brothers and sisters as well as with non-Christians. Unfortunately, many Christians are hurt by other Christians to the point of them wanting to leave a church congregation altogether. You would think what kids are taught on the playground of "play nice with one another" would be learned by the time they become adults, Christ-loving adults at that!

The problem comes when people equate Christians with perfection. Only God is perfect. Christians are still fallible human beings who may be working on their sanctification but will never achieve perfection. Every Christian is running a race (Heb. 12:1), some in different stages of the race than others. Unfortunately, this will sometimes lead to conflict, hurt feelings, jealousy, rudeness, and overall sinfulness even within the church.

Hurt people hurt people. It's important to distinguish between fallible people and an infallible God. Not going to church at all because of hurt caused by fellow "Christians" is like not driving ever again because you got into an accident in the past. Discernment will allow you to make the best decision as to whether you should still go to that specific church or if there is a better option for you. Keep in mind that a perfect church does not exist, so if that is your goal while you are church shopping, you will be in a perpetual search.

Despite the struggles that come with two humans trying to play nice with one another, Christians need to be built up and encouraged by other Christians. This is an important need for the Body of Christ from 1 Corinthians 12 that discusses how the Body has different but important functions. We do not need to all look and act the same. Christians bring different human and spiritual gifts to the corporate gathering, all to be used for God's glory.

> *Just as a body, though one, has many parts, but all its many parts form one body, so it is with Christ. For we were all baptized by one Spirit so as to form one body- whether Jews or Gentiles, slave or free- and we were all given the one Spirit to drink. Even so the body is not made up of one part but of many (1 Cor. 12:12-14).*

The Bible tells us to "encourage one another" multiple times (2 Cor. 3:11, 1 Thess. 4:18, 1 Thess. 5:11, Heb. 3:13). We should encourage each other so that "no one is hardened by sin's deceitfulness" (Heb. 3:13). The Christian walk is hard enough with our enemy trying to thwart us at every step. We need encouragement from like-minded believers in Christ who will be there to pray with us, encourage us, and strengthen us.

Church is much more than attendance. We should not *go* to church; we *are* the church as believers. God does not need to reside in a temple anymore for His power to be revealed. We are the Temple of God as believers in Christ (1 Cor. 3:16). Our actions all week long can show Jesus to believers and unbelievers alike. Our gathering should simply be used for corporate worship of God and edification of the Body of believers. The calling of *being* the church equips us to do life with both believers and unbelievers, to be there to pray, to help with needs, to give of our time, to die to ourselves.

FELLOWSHIP

My wife and I were involved with the church for many years while, at the same time, we were missing a deeper connection with Christian friends throughout the week. We "knew" a lot of people and were involved in activities that kept us busy in ministry, but something was missing. My wife was more aware of this than I was; I was not realizing there was an open hole for fellowship in our lives. I could "get by" okay without it. My personality usually requires me to have down time without other people (not including my immediate family). However, my wife and I led a few marriage groups at our church, and out of that grew a wonderful fellowship group with four other families.

We all had a need for this in our lives, and we made a concerted effort to meet weekly to discuss our lives and the sermon from the weekend. While there were growing pains and apprehensiveness to get over, our fellowship quickly grew into something valuable for each member. The group became like a second family, and we lovingly call each other "framily" (friend/family). We do life together, we attend birthday parties, celebrate holidays, and the men and women have separate times of fellowship to discuss more personal issues.

Is this a solution for fellowship for everyone out there? No. But I cannot discount the impact it has had on the lives involved. I feel it is an important aspect of relationships among the church and is more than just "having friends." Having a group to challenge you spiritually and be there when the enemy comes attacking is invaluable. I have seen other fellowship groups in the church withstand attacks that no single person would be equipped to do without the power of the Holy Spirit.

When disaster strikes, they are quickly surrounded in prayer, support, and food. I have heard the testimony of men who have said that, if they did not have the support of a fellowship of believers at the time of physical or spiritual attacks, they would have quickly regenerated back to destructive habits or left the faith altogether.

I think there is a difference in having a deeper fellowship with five to ten people separate from being involved in hundreds of lives. If it is your desire to have this type of fellowship but you do not have it yet, start by praying. Things like this do not usually happen overnight; my wife and I were involved in ministries and poured out of ourselves to many people for many years before it came to fruition for us. Do not wait for the church or pastor to put something together for you. Whether you have a fellowship group like I described, a covenant group, accountability group, mentor meetings, or just people to "do life" with, find what works for you and your situation.

Pray, be involved, and put yourself out there as scary as it may seem. Be the type of brother or sister in Christ that you want to fellowship with. Personalities will clash, emotions may run wild, some people just do not harmonize well, and that is okay. You can still love and *show* love for your fellow brothers and sisters in Christ without having deep relationships with them.

I DO...EVERY DAY

Discernment with our words in marriage was discussed in a previous chapter; discernment in marriage with the goal of preserving the relationship is what I want to discuss here, realizing I will only be touching the surface on the topic.

A marriage takes work—hard work from both parties. A husband and wife should die to themselves daily, sacrificing for one another and the family. If someone enters into a marriage and tries to live under the guise of getting only his or her own needs met whether it is financial, sexual, emotional, or spiritual, without meeting the needs of his or her partner, the marriage will have a high chance of failure. Each person in the marriage covenant should wake up each day and think of ways they can honor his or her spouse, dying to his or her own will and desires in order to please the other. This is not a sustainable model if it is one-sided. If both are servants to one another, you can have a beautiful relationship that is honoring to God.

Most days, however, will not be an equal output of effort from both sides into the marriage. One day, a spouse might be stressed and need to be picked up emotionally by the other. Later, the tables will turn, and it will be the other person's job to uplift. There is a give and take, an ebb and flow to marriage that allows for the relationship to be strengthened in spite of weakness without letting the weakness define the marriage. No couple can give 100% of their energy to a relationship every day. Instead of 100/100, it might be 50/50, 80/20, or even 20/20. In the latter case, the couple must rely on God to get them through and allow for a recharge in priorities and focus.

In order to grow your relationship as a married couple, you need to use discernment as a way of making the right decisions and consider what the outcomes will be for your decisions; communication is key.

It's important to "date" your spouse. When my wife tells me that we need a date night and we don't make a concerted effort to make that happen (even harder with younger kids), weeks and even months may pass, and then, I notice a sadness come out at times when she doesn't feel cherished. We might even fail to connect on other levels or create frivolous conflict simply by not prioritizing the needs of each other. If your spouse is open with you about his or her needs, be grateful, first of all, that he or she is communicating with you; secondly, you must take action to ensure he or she feels like his or her needs matter.

Much of the failure to communicate does not come from verbal but rather tonal and nonverbal cues. "When a person says, 'I don't feel loved by you,' or 'You never listen to me anymore,' typically they aren't talking about words; they are talking about actions."[2] Rarely will both spouses want to communicate at the exact same level.

My wife and I both struggle with communicating how we are feeling and what we are stressed out about. We like to internalize, sometimes to a fault until it builds up like a volcano inside us that erupts at the worst possible time. Knowing this is a struggle, we have to make it a focus to find time away from the kids, to "force" ourselves to talk about what is bothering us or what we are stressed out about.

My wife does a good job of prompting me, "Tell me three things you are stressed out about right now." This opens the doorway to communication that I would have probably not sought out if it wasn't for her asking. When I notice my wife is stressed out about something, I ask, "What's wrong?" If she replies quickly with "nothing," then I know we either need to make time to talk or I need to follow up with her later on, after she has had time to process her feelings.

Every marriage is unique, but it's important to be able to analyze (like I just did for mine) what problems usually arise and why. What pitfalls take place due to personality, situational, or spiritual factors, and what steps can be taken to avoid them before they start?

Building your relationship together in marriage should be rooted in Jesus, the foundation of our faith. If you are growing separately but not together in your faith, there is a missing piece to your relationship. The Bible says we are "one" with our spouses (Mark 10:8). We are not only one physically but spiritually and emotionally as well.

Prayer cannot be understated for what it can bring to a marital relationship. Francis Chan clarifies as follows, "Sincere and concentrated prayer will do infinitely more than any human strategy for a happy marriage."[3]

On the other end of the spectrum, if someone in a marriage does not focus on his personal relationship with Jesus, it does a disservice to the growth of the couple. Each partner should have his or her personal time with God, reading, praying, and growing in his or her faith. Then each individual can bring something to the equation when they meet and join together.

Picture the husband who does not read the Bible or grow in his faith in any way. The wife has to drag him to church, force him to pray, and the only spiritual exercise he gets is when she initiates it. This "man" (I use man in quotes because he is acting spiritually immature) would be a detriment to the relationship; he is only being dragged along by his wife who has to pour out to him and, in turn, finds herself drained because of it. If both parties are filling their spiritual reservoir on their own time, they will have an outpouring of the Holy Spirit to share with one another.

Remember group projects in school? There always seemed to be one person on the team who never held up his end of the deal. Each student would be given an individual piece of the project to accomplish on his or her own time. Timelines would be established so that all members would know when they needed to complete their portion of the project.

What inevitably would happen is that one person (or more) would not complete it in time, would not communicate with the group, and the rest of the group would scramble to cover the last end of the deal. Sound familiar? In a perfect scenario, all group members would accomplish exactly what they were assigned, and when the project was brought together with all pieces intact and timely, it would result in an excelling grade.

The same can be said for a marital relationship. Both are called to a "group project," if you will. This group project lasts the rest of your lives. Each has a role to play. If there is a lack on one side, the other should pick him or her up. This will happen from time to time when a spouse is facing a struggle; the stronger mate will pick her up and help her get to a place of strength. This should be the exception and not the rule. If it is a continual thing, the stronger spouse might get tired, worn out, or unmotivated to keep pulling his mate up when he does not get anything in return.

The goal behind saying "I do...every day" is to put the *effort* in that will keep your marriage going for decades longer. If you think of any sports analogy, a player cannot rest on his accomplishments. He cannot say, "I practiced last week," "I won the championship three years ago," and "I had the best season of my career last year."

A married partner cannot say similar things like: "I prayed with my spouse every day during that one year of our marriage when we had health issues," "Our connection spiritually was at an all-time high during our first year of marriage," or "We read that book together a while back and really connected." All those statements look back at the past. As a married couple, it's important to look at the present and future. Are the steps you are putting into practice *today* going to further your relationship or destroy it? It's simply not enough to show up to the game!

Using discernment in your marital relationship will allow you to analyze your words and actions as to whether they are being used for building up or tearing down. Great marriages do not "just happen," and love is "not enough." The same can be said about bad marriages. They do not "just happen;" They are a conscious effort by one or both parties to not work on the marriage and neglect the commitment they made. True commitment is dying to yourself, putting Jesus as head of the relationship, and serving your spouse's needs before your own.

CHAPTER 8 REFLECTION AND DISCUSSION QUESTIONS

1. What lessons have you learned from poor relationships in the past?

2. When you were single, did you use your time wisely in preparing for a spouse? If you still are single, how can you prepare yourself for a spouse?

3. How do you accept the good with the bad concerning your spouse without letting it lead to abuse?

4. Why are friendships important in the Body of Christ? How have you used friendships to grow in your walk with Jesus?

5. Why is communication important in a relationship/ marriage? How have you seen the lack of communication hurt a relationship?

6. What does saying "I do every day" in your marriage mean to you?

CHAPTER 9:
DISCERNMENT IN PARENTING

Parenting is a journey. I doubt if any first-time parent feels fully equipped and "qualified" to be a parent. Despite the thousands of books out there and the wisdom from God given to us in the Bible on parenting, no parent parents perfectly. We grow in knowledge and understanding through the journey. We make mistakes.

Being a parent to your unique children requires understanding of them as individuals. There are universal parenting guidelines to help along the way, but a good parent will apply them in the context of his or her situation, marriage, environment, and child.

Good parenting, like marriage, takes effort. It requires a focused effort; it does not just happen. With two parents, it requires them to be a cohesive team. The father should not try to subvert his wife's authority and vice versa. Parenting strategy and discipline should be an agreed upon topic before children are even in the picture. How to raise your children spiritually should also be agreed upon; otherwise, there will be strife among the couple and confusion among the children.

Discernment in parenting calls upon the Holy Spirit inside us to make the right decisions in the moment. Knowing when to pray for or with your children when all you want to do is yell at them for something they did wrong is a God-given ability that supersedes our natural emotions.

RULES VS. GRACE

The rules parents make in their household are unique to each family, and you have the authority to set them in place as long as you are not breaking any governmental laws. The rules you make should be made with wisdom and cohesiveness as a parental unit. A parent provokes a child to anger and rebellion when rules are arbitrary, inconsistent, without reference to God's truth, and enforced with power instead of love.[1]

As parents, it is even more important to lead by example. Using "Do what I say, not what I do" diminishes your authority and leaves children thinking that the rules don't apply when you get older. In Titus 2:7, Paul instructs "in everything set them an example by doing what is good. In your teaching show integrity..." It's hard for someone of any age to follow a leader that is hypocritical or expects things that he would not want to do.

Some common ways parents do not lead by example are: asking for communication but not giving any in return, telling children to calm down without showing them how, asking kids to admit their mistakes while rationalizing their own, stressing the importance of financial management without being able to maintain a budget, and explaining how important God is without ever opening a Bible.

If a parent finds he made a mistake, he should be wise enough to admit he was wrong. Our kids make mistakes all the time as they learn how to function as human beings. When we give our kids grace, they will give us grace as well if we are humble and ask for forgiveness as needed.

I KNOW YOU

Parenting is not just about the rules; it's about relationship. You cannot have a relationship with someone that you command around and do not spend time with in order to know that person's heart, motivations, fears, joys, failures, and loves. Building a relationship takes time; it takes being present in your children's lives. Parents who do not take advantage of times they have to build their relationships with their children but who let distractions continually hinder relational growth will usually result in children who do not feel valued.

Children have things they love to do with each parent, either individually or collectively. My wife and I make a point to also spend time individually with each child. We do "daddy/daughter" and "mommy/son" date nights to show each child he or she is cherished. I also have specific activities I do with only my son as a part of "male bonding," and with my daughter, it's all about her tea parties and stuffed animals.

Children are very perceptive. They know when they are not important or valued in a parent's life. They know the difference between obligation and celebration when a parent spends time with them. They can discern the difference between a parent showing them love and them saying "I love you" at bedtime. A parent's life is busy, but the time you do spend with your children should be quality time even if, on a particular day, you only have ten minutes. Ask them questions; use the dinner table as a means of conversation. Many families, including mine, ask during dinner what everyone's favorite and least favorite thing done that day was.

TEACH WITH WORDS AND ACTIONS

Proverbs 22:6 says to "train up a child in the way he should go and when he is old he will not depart from it." This verse in Proverbs directs us be our children's first teachers. Don't wait for someone else to do it and also validate what they are learning from other sources. I find it interesting that Proverbs says, "When he is *old* he will not depart from it." This could be interpreted that it is a possibility that the child *could* depart from it *before* they are old. If you establish a foundation of Bible-based truth, even if your child turns away from it early in life, you have to trust in God that the foundation you established will always be with him or her, whether he or she chooses to follow it or not. And let God do the rest while you faithfully pray.

Always remember that your children have free will just as God allows us to have free will as His children. A child's actions later in life are not always reflective of the quality of parenting that child received. There are direct correlations with poor parenting and poor decisions made by their children, good parenting and good decisions; however, this is not always 100% the case.

I constantly compare my childhood with that of my children. I compare where I was during each stage of life. I compare what I learned from my parents vs. what I am teaching my children. I think back to what pets I had, what shows I watched, what toys I played with, what friends I had, where we went on vacation, and how we connected as a family. I think these thoughts are natural—for parents to compare what they knew growing up with how their children's upbringing is.

I need to have discernment, knowing my children are different than I was, my circumstances are different, the opportunities my children have might be different, and they have different wants and needs.

Not only that, but society, culture, and technology are vastly different from when I was growing up which adds different complexities to a child's development.

My childhood was great, but I also cannot and should not try to copy every aspect and superimpose each onto my children. I should take the good parts, the values, the lessons, the learnings, and absolutely share them with my children when it is the right time to do so. I do my children a disservice if I compare them to how I acted at their age or what I was interested in and expect the same from them. I do not honor their uniqueness that God has given them by expecting clones of myself.

If you had a negative childhood, this is even more important. Too often, as parents, we copy "what we know" and not what we *should* do. It takes effort to seek out resources to learn a new way of parenting than what you were shown. There's a reason that sins of the parent follow through to generations.

Horrible vices from a parent like drunkenness, anger, sexual immorality, drug abuse, laziness, and selfish ambition often sneak their way into children, but why? Parents, for the most part, do not start their parenting journey by saying "I really want to install this sin into my children." The problem in this case is that children learn by seeing and are vulnerable to what is being modeled.

Unless the power of Jesus is allowed to intervene in a parent's life or through the child breaking the cycle, it will have a propensity to continue. New lives can be had through the work that Jesus accomplished on the cross and with His resurrection. It takes a conscious effort for a parent to be aware of his shortcomings and his vices and make tangible steps to diminish their impact or eliminate them altogether. Parents need to daily submit to Jesus and find accountability with others who will keep them from slipping into old habits. When you are in the trenches of life and the enemy starts to attack, you either succumb to the pressure and revert to *what* you know or you stand strong in your faith and fix your eyes on *Who* you know.

SACRIFICE

Parents know the meaning of sacrifice when it comes to their children, especially when raising younger children. From sleepless nights, lack of energy, and usually little to no recognition, giving up wants for the children's needs seems to be a daily occurrence for parents.

Parents willingly do this because of the value they place on their children. Our Heavenly Father is our example in this when He placed infinite value on His creation by sending His son, Jesus, to die for us and save us from the consequences of sin and death.

Discernment as a parent when it comes to sacrifice goes above and beyond not going to see a new movie on Saturday so you can go to your child's baseball game or going to a fast food place your children love *again* so they can get a kid's meal. Parents need to look at the big picture. Sometimes, it's hard to keep straight what month it is let alone knowing what the impact of the actions you are taking now for your children will be five, ten, or fifteen years down the road.

Parents may live with the focus on birthday to birthday, holiday to holiday, school year to summer, but parents also need to have a goal in mind for what the future holds for their children while also coming to terms with never really knowing what is in store because only God does. This does not mean pushing your child toward a specific degree, career, or sport against his will. For me, as a parent, my goal is to set up my children for success based on the foundation I have built in their lives and allow them to hear from God and have discernment on the direction they should take.

Aligning your will with God's as a parent requires you to step outside of what you know as a parent, what was modeled to you, or what you have read in a book. Hearing God's voice allows you to understand a little bit of the Kingdom-focus that you are building when you raise your children, to speak life into their lives by prayer and encouragement. The benefit of this sacrifice comes as a parent when you see a glimpse of the future benefit of what you are doing today for your children.

The decision of what and why to sacrifice for your children will be unique to each parent and requires a thorough God-inspired analysis of your personal situation. Not every situation is the same. Sometimes, sacrifice as a parent is thrust upon you with little choice. Situations like divorce or health issues may put you in a season of sacrifice where you may not see the long-term benefits. Even in those situations, calling up discernment for God's direction is more crucial than ever.

Let me give you a couple of personal examples of the importance of high-level parental sacrifice for the long-term benefits of my children.

My wife and I decided early on that the best thing to do for our children was for her to stay home with them as soon as they were born. God had blessed us to the point where she could give up her job as a teacher and focus on our family. We analyzed the finances, prayed about our decisions, and even read a couple books, but the choice was clear it was in the best interest of our family. This is not to say that there was not a sacrifice to be made; we had to create and stick to a new budget. The same need for discernment took place when my son was approaching school age. We saw that he was gifted in many subjects and would need to be challenged by more advanced material than kindergarten. However, his maturity level was appropriate for his age, so moving him up a year or two in school would do a disservice to him and his social development.

Home-schooling was the answer for us. The benefits of these decisions for my son and my daughter many years later are quite evident. They have been shown a love by their parents that could not have easily been replaced by a stranger. They are able to hear about God on a daily basis through the material we use in school that would have never come across in public school.

I am not trying to recommend home-schooling to every parent in every situation. However, for us, it was the best decision, and the fruits of that decision will impact my children for years to come. There have absolutely been challenges and struggles. It has been a sacrifice for us, especially my wife. She gave up a career and her personal aspirations to spend most of her waking hours with two small humans we each helped create. We see the connection with our parental sacrifice and the benefits for our children. We continue to use discernment every year and re-analyze if it is the best decision for our children.

The second example on sacrifice is fostering. I have seen the sacrifice of many families firsthand, including my sister and brother-in-law who decided to foster after their biological children reached adulthood. I have seen these parents of foster kids give of everything they have for "random" children, who they quickly love as their own, in order for them to have comfort, safety, and a semblance of normalcy in their traumatic lives.

The sacrifices that are made of time, money, emotions, and, sometimes, sanity are hard but gladly given because these parents see the big picture. I have seen some of these same families needing discernment when the opportunity has come to adopt these children. Although it can be one of the biggest decisions parents need to make, I have seen it made without question; they gladly allow this child to share in their lives, to be called their son or daughter, and to share in their inheritance. It is a model of how Christ loves us and how He sacrificed for us so that we can be called His sons and daughters (John 1:12), though we are not deserving of that honor, and we now share the inheritance of God's Kingdom (Col. 1:12).

Most parents sacrifice for their children. Whatever the sacrifice you make as a parent, it is important to understand why you do what you do. Sacrifices are not as noble as they sound if they are based on the selfish dreams or needs of the parent without benefitting the child. If there is not a connection with the positive results that you hope to achieve or that you pray God achieves, it could lead to resentment and frustration.

STAND IN THE GAP

Some parents who want to be their children's friend more than their authority end up letting them have everything they want, allowing their children to make the rules. This is not to say that you cannot be your child's friend, but the hierarchy of authority needs to be recognized and respected by both sides. When parents do not enact discipline, they are actually doing their children a huge disservice.

Parents are called to discipline their children just as God disciplines those He loves. "'Do not make light of the Lord's discipline, and do not lose heart when he rebukes you'" (Heb. 12:5). Proverbs 18:24 tells us that "the one who loves their children is careful to discipline them." Parents need to make sure that any discipline they enact on their children is out of love for them, not anger. Even if the punishment is severe, a child should not question whether her parent loves her or not, although she will undoubtedly be upset. The love for my children never changes or diminishes even though there have been times when I did not *like* them very much in a moment!

Many children will not fully realize the love their parent had for them in the midst of punishment until they are adults or a parent themselves, and that is ok. This does not change the responsibility of a parent to guide and direct his or her children's paths.

Nobody understands your child better than you do. Using discernment in parenting is crucial every day to understand the heart of your children and what type of direction is specifically needed for them. Parents should provide their children with discipline through means of training, correction, verbal instruction, and punishment. The purpose in discipline should always be to guide and impart wisdom during the process. The means will change as the children mature in age.

During the younger stages of a child's life, parents are simply focused on things to keep him or her safe, out of traffic, from eating poisonous things, and in obedience to instruction. As the child matures, he or she should be allowed to make more choices on his or her own and learn from the consequences.

God as our Heavenly Father did not create us to be robots, and we cannot expect our children to be either. We have the ultimate source of our guidance in the Bible and the Holy Spirit. Parents should fight for their child's very soul to the point that the child has a clear picture of what he or she is choosing and why. If a child chooses poorly, the parents will be disappointed but should be comforted by the fact that they did all they could in training and instructing the child up to the very point of the decision.

The High Priest Eli in the Bible is a good example of bad parenting. Eli's two sons, Hophni and Phinehas, were described as wicked scoundrels (1 Sam. 2:12). They had no respect for their position as priests and took advantage of it. They kept the sacrifices for themselves and did not follow the rules as to what part they were allowed to take. They treated the Lord's offering with contempt (v. 17). They slept with the women who served the Lord at the tent where the sacrifices were being made (v. 22). Eli did rebuke his sons by telling them not to do such an evil thing by sinning against the Lord, but they did not listen to him (v. 25).

Reading this so far, one might think, "Well, Eli tried, and his sons didn't listen. It's not his fault..." Picking up in Chapter 3, Samuel was awakened by the Lord and given a prophecy against Eli and his sons. God said he would judge Eli's family forever because of the sin Eli *knew* about and that he "failed to restrain them" (v.

3:13). Eli's sons were later killed in battle (1 Sam. 4:11), and Eli fell off a chair and broke his neck upon hearing the news (1 Sam. 4:18).

Eli had the power as High Priest to condemn the actions of his sons and remove them from the priestly office. Was he afraid of the dishonor to his family name? Eli loved them as a father, but he tried to reason with them instead of rebuking them. He had a duty and responsibility to enforce God's laws in order to maintain the holiness of the nation.

Eli was too passive and too weak. His sons were already hardened sinners by the time he mentioned something to them. The time for their teaching, training, and parenting was long gone. Eli's sons concluded that God was just like their father and would not take action against their blatant sin. They were horribly wrong.

What can be learned from this example is that, as parents, we should never give up on our children. It's not enough to simply "say our peace;" instead, we are accountable to our children before God. Now if we have minor children, we have more authority. We are the authority to our children as long as they live in our home. With authority comes the power.

Children who do not obey an earthly authority usually have a hard time obeying a Heavenly one. Parents must make a stand for their minor children when they are on the verge of making a terrible decision. Parents need to be the voice of reason. Yes, children should learn from their mistakes, but if it is something that can be avoided, why not? However, once a poor decision is made, there must be consequences mixed with love and forgiveness.

Parents of adult children have an important role as well. By this time, the lessons have been taught, the model set before them. Now you must pray, *really* pray, every day for your children to make the right decisions. You must stand in the gap before God and your children, being ready to come beside them when they ask for advice, praying faithfully for their fulfillment of God's calling on their lives.

If a child, minor or adult, seems lost, a parent should not lose heart but be ready to receive him or her with open arms like the parent in the story of the prodigal son (Luke 15). In this story, a son asks for his half of the inheritance from his father. He runs off and lives a wild life and spends all the money. He lives among the pigs, starving and penniless. The son eventually comes to his senses and decides to go back to his father to live as a servant. The father sees him coming back, runs toward him, throws his arms around and embraces his lost son.

The father orders the best robe to be put on him with a ring on his finger and sandals on his feet. He orders the best fatted calf to be killed to celebrate a feast "for this son of mine was dead and is alive again; he was lost and is found" (Luke 15:24).

This story is an example to all parents to never give up on their children. If your children disappoint you and make bad decisions, trust that God loves them even more than you do. Kneel in the gap between their sins and forgiveness, praying fervently for the day when they will return to the foundation that was laid before them during their childhood.

To say that parenting is a huge responsibility is an understatement. Being a godly parent does not always guarantee having godly kids and vice versa. The rewards of having children far outweigh the struggles and pain you will face as a parent. Just one tender eye lock, one "I love you," one "thank you," one squeeze of your hand from your child on a bad day is enough to go through a battlefield for him because he is worth it and he means more to you than life itself!

CHAPTER 9 REFLECTION AND DISCUSSION QUESTIONS

1. What lessons did you learn about parenting from your parents, and how have you applied them in your adult life?

2. How have you grown on your parenting journey, regardless of the stage you are in?

3. What does the balance of rules vs. grace look like in your home? Why is a balance needed between the two?

4. In what ways are you intentional to build a relationship with each of your children?

5. How does someone who had a negative childhood not allow those influences to affect his or her parenting style?

6. What are the major sacrifices you have made or are currently making for your children? What is the goal you had/have in making them?

7. How is discipline as a parent correlated with how God disciplines His children? How has discipline changed for you as a parent during the different stages of your child's life?

CHAPTER 10:
DISCERNMENT IN CAREER

There should not be a disconnect between the vocation we choose and having Spirit-led discernment about what that should be. Some people know from a young age what they want to do with their careers. Others, like me, tend to "go with the flow." I went through college without any real career goals other than to get my degree. After completing a business degree, specifically marketing, a management role opened up right after college, and I jumped at the chance to make a good salary. God has blessed my career and given me the strength and fortitude to do my job well and provide for my family.

It's important to note that, no matter what you do, whether you are a fry cook or a CEO, God does not want you to separate your job from your relationship with Him. These are not mutually exclusive. The Bible upholds any line of work that is honest and good (Titus 3:1; cp. Gen. 2:15; Neh. 2:18) and does not contradict the gospel (Acts 16:16–18; 19:23–27).[1]

The goal of this chapter is to see your job in light of the bigger picture with the goal of bringing honor and glory to Jesus in whatever you do.

THE MOST TOYS

You may have heard the saying, "He who dies with the most toys...still dies." Too often, the goal of our career is to build up for ourselves a comfortable lifestyle that we will someday enjoy after retirement. Someday, we will give back money to God when we have "enough." Someday, we will enjoy our spouses after we retire. Someday, we will volunteer at the church when we finally get weekends off. Someday, we will relax. Someday, we will get enough sleep. Someday...sometimes... never comes.

Colossians 3:17 instructs us, "Whatever you do, whether in word or deed, do it all in the name of the Lord Jesus, giving thanks to God the Father through him." Just a few verses later, verse 23 says, "Whatever you do, work at it with all your heart, as working for the Lord, not for human masters." I use this verse with my son about the chores he needs to do because serving as unto the Lord in small things will grow as the same principles are applied to larger things.

Everything we do we should do with excellence. Our work ethic is a reflection of Jesus; if we are lazy or not giving our all, it reflects back on Jesus, Who is our ultimate authority. He is more concerned with our attitude and faithfulness than the actual task we are accomplishing. Even if it is not a job where you are planning on staying, don't job abandon, don't show up late, and don't slander those around you; don't let your witness be tarnished because you are discontented.

Sometimes, God calls people out of their vocation into a purpose He has for them. Take a look at Moses, Gideon, Paul, Nehemiah, and many more in the Bible. Other times, we are called to be faithful "for a season" where we are. Sometimes, this season is our whole life. I know many people who have a job but also have a thriving non-profit on the side who make a huge impact in the communities they are in. Others I know have a side business that eventually becomes their main focus. It all depends on the stage of life you are in and having discernment about whether the timing is right for you and your family.

BATTLEGROUND

Your workplace is your battleground, your mission field. Too often, Christians treat work as a separate thing. They incorrectly feel they must only *go* to a foreign country to be engaged in the mission field. Wherever you are placed, *that* is your mission field. Our enemy is real; Satan tries to gain ground wherever he can because he knows his time is short (Rev. 12:12). Whether you work in fast food, an office building, or at home, you are called to take authority over that place by praying and showing love to those around you (employees *and* customers).

Take ground in your battleground. In taking ground for Jesus in your workplace, I am referring to honoring Jesus in all you do, being a witness to others through your integrity, and showing the love of Jesus to other people through your interactions.

Maybe you need to get to work early once a week and pray over the building, the doorways, the offices, and the people who will be coming to work. Pray God's will to be done in their lives and that you honor God in all of your transactions with them. Do not underestimate the power of these actions. It's important for Christians to not just "go through the motions" with their jobs. They need to focus on fulfilling the Great Commission (Matt. 28:19), which, in turn, could lead to more fulfillment in their jobs. When you see the connection with your job and God's Kingdom, it can help avoid discontentment.

You may think something like, "My job just pays the bills, but I can't wait to leave it each and every day." Some questions to aid in your discernment of your vocation might be: Does God have something better for you? Have you prayed to be used by God where you are? Is God calling you to move on to something greater or be faithful in the moment?

C. Peter Wagner, author of *The Church in the Workplace: How God's People Can Transform Society* says that Christians need to be active in their faith in the workplace:

> *We live in two different cultures. Christians need to be like missionaries, taking their faith into a culture that is different than the church. Sometimes believers try to transfer the piety of the church into the workplace, and that doesn't work. We have to adapt to the workplace culture.* [2]

Your coworkers may never have been to church and may never plan to go. Your actions may either *lead* them in the direction of Jesus or further their resolve of believing "religion" and Jesus are not for them.

IDENTITY AT WORK

We cannot turn on and turn off our Christian faith depending on the circumstances we are in. We need to be Christians 100% of the time. This does not mean that we need to be verbally witnessing non-stop, but it does mean that we cannot live two lives.

God does not want "fair-weather" followers. This happens a lot in sports, and I am also guilty of it. A hometown sports team that I have not followed all year makes it to the playoffs, and suddenly, I dust off my old hat in the closet and watch every game with intentness. If the same team has a poor year, I may not even watch one game.

Fair-weather fans put value on their sports team when it is exciting or when the stakes are high. Fair-weather Christians treat their faith the same way.

They might hide it when they are at their jobs and act however they want all week long. However, in church, camp, or a Christian concert, they put their "team colors" on and raise their hands and sing extra loudly... maybe.

Christian is a term meaning "follower of Christ." Our new identity is bought with the precious blood of Christ. An identity is not something that you can turn on or off; you just are! Peter writes to "God's elect" and exhorts them in their new identity.

> But you are a chosen people, a royal priesthood, a holy nation, God's special possession, that you may declare the praises of him who called you out of darkness into his wonderful light. Once you were not a people, but now you are the people of God; once you had not received mercy, but now you have received mercy (1 Pet. 2:9-10).

God sees us the same regardless if we are in a board meeting, running a register, cooking a hamburger, or mixing concrete. We are His special people with a high calling to bring honor to our heavenly "CEO," if you will.

VALUE YOUR VALUES

How do we know when we are in the wrong vocation? Using discernment will reveal certain companies or industries to be a definite "no" for the Christian based on the types of services or products they provide. Other companies might look good on the outside, but once you are in the company for an amount of time, you might realize that there are some immoral and unethical practices going on. You may suddenly have a new boss who is asking you to falsify some numbers, to lie on paperwork, or to make a deal "under the table." You should not have to compromise your values for the company you work for.

John Maxwell has a book on this subject called *There's No Such Thing As "Business" Ethics.* In it, he presents the idea that there should not be a difference between Business Ethics and Ethics; you are either an ethical person or you are not. To assume there is a difference between how we act in business versus our personal lives allows us to lead two different lives. In the book, he says:

> *Ethics + Competence is a winning equation. In contrast, people who continually attempt to test the edge of ethics inevitably go over that edge. Shortcuts never pay off in the long run. It may be possible to fool people for a season, but in the long haul, their deeds will catch up with them because the truth does come out.*[3]

Sometimes, you will not be called to leave a job but to be the light in the darkness. You can make a decision to not break the rules and your ethics even if you are surrounded by it. It takes discernment and direction from God on when it is the right time to move on.

Tony Evans, author of *Kingdom Man,* writes about a time he worked at a bus station loading buses. Everyone there would take turns punching his or her coworkers back into work while the other person slept, effectively stealing from the company. Tony made the stand by not doing this and faced the ridicule, isolation, and emotional and physical ramifications of these actions.

Management came to him and told him that they were aware of the actions and that he did not participate in them. He was given a management position, and his pay doubled. He summarizes this experience by saying:

> *If you want to be great—if you want to be blessed—take advantage of every opportunity to demonstrate that you fear God both with internal opportunities and external opportunities, holding Him in highest honor and esteem in every aspect of your life.*[4]

Pastor Matt Chandler spoke at a "Work as Worship" retreat. There he discussed how entrepreneurs and business owners can use their gifts, talents, and connections for the Kingdom of God. They may have a regular customer base, but they can do the work of God because they get to direct the focus on the business. Matt says, "My hope is for you to see that your job is not secular and church is sacred... but when you head to the office, you are doing God stuff, you are doing gospel stuff."[5]

As a Christian, where you work is not just a "job." It is a platform, it is a calling, and it is an extension of your current faith to use discernment on when and how to make it known to others, to be an example in a sinful world, and to live out our commission of knowing Jesus and making Him known!

FAMILY BALANCE

Working and finding balance in your family can be a Catch-22. After all, you are working *for* your family, but sometimes, it feels like you rarely get to see them. Your family needs to eat; they need the security that a stable job provides. The success in your career will not only strengthen your family's finances but also secure your future, right?

It is a noble accomplishment to sacrifice for your family. To work long hours, to give up personal wants, to face the stress of work daily to bring home the paycheck that will provide. The use of discernment will allow you to decide when it becomes too much. Each situation will be different, so you must use God's leading to help you decide if you are really working for your family or for yourself. Are you trying to climb the corporate ladder because it is what is best for your family, or will it hurt your relationship with your kids and spouse?

When I was first married, we had just bought a house. We were excited about the move, and we were closer to family and our church. At my job, I was offered a higher position, something that I always wanted. It would, however, require us to move about three hours away... away from our new house that was a new build, away from our support network of family and the church.

It was a tough decision that I prayed with my wife over, but we said no. I turned down that which I wanted for that which we needed. In hindsight, it was absolutely the right decision. It would have led to a lot more stress, and we would not have made the friends or had our family as heavily invested in the lives of our children.

I was never given the opportunity for that specific promotion again, though, and in a way that hurts my pride. However, knowing that I made the best decision for my family strengthens me as a man of God. God has blessed us in many ways. Career opportunities will come and go. A goal of Christian discernment is to be able to say no to the good so you can say yes to the best!

You may be in a season where you hate your job, you and your family are stressed, and you work long hours trying to achieve a goal of a certain dollar amount or title. I would encourage you to not isolate yourself from your children or your spouse. Pray with your spouse on directions for what to do. Maybe you do need to stay at your job. How can you make the best of it, and how can you stay engaged with your family so that you are not a stranger to them because they barely see you?

Kids need to know that they are safe, that their parents love them no matter what. Children should not have to stress about finances or job security. Make sure you bring the joy of the Lord to your family even if you do not "feel" like it. Let them know that they are more important than the job that is taking you away from them. With prayer, discernment, and agreement as a married team, you will know when the time is right to make the change.

MINISTRY

I want to briefly write to those whose careers are their ministry. Whether you are a pastor or staff at a church, leading a Christian volunteer organization, or a full-time missionary, you are in an often-enviable position among Christians, being able to work in an area that has direct Kingdom significance. The pressures of doing this, however, are often a lot higher than a secular career. After all, you feel more like you answer to a higher authority even if you have a human supervisor.

This can lead to feelings of doubt and unworthiness because you know what you struggle with better than anyone else. But who can you talk to about your sin, your fears, your doubts? Oftentimes, that list is small. Why would you want to appear weak or sinful to your staff or congregation? Wouldn't your witness be tarnished if they knew you did *that* or thought *that*?

My first point is that you *need* an outlet of accountability with someone you trust. This would preferably not only be your spouse. You should be open and honest with your spouse, but someone else needs to come beside you to lift you up. This should be someone that understands your role, someone who isn't asking for the responsibility, and someone who loves you no matter what.

Pastors that feel they have no outlet often succumb to the greatest vices. There's a reason that you see so many fall away due to sin; there is a huge target on their backs from the enemy! They need to be aware of the fact that they cannot bottle up all their emotions, fears, and doubts... it will eventually overtake them. I've had pastors tell me that counseling alone provides a huge sense of disturbance in their spirits. They hear terrible stories of the worst of the sinful flesh, and they have no outlet on how to express their emotions. They have to be strong for their congregation. An accountability partner or group is vital to *any* Christian but, especially, to someone in ministry!

My second point is that you need a time to refresh, unwind, and decompress *away* from your ministry. This can be in the form of a sabbatical or just very strategic vacation taking. Wayne Cordeiro wrote a great book on this called *Leading on Empty*. In it, he says, "Solitude is a chosen separation for refining your soul. Isolation is what you crave when you neglect the first."[6]

Burnout is a common symptom in ministry of neglecting to take time away to recharge. What may feel like a "waste of time" or neglect of your ministry is actually a benefit to it. You cannot help others when you are running on empty; eventually, the fuel tank will run out if it is not replenished. Only by filling yourself up with a renewal of your spirit can you once again give freely to others. It takes discernment to be aware of the signs of burnout and your personal risk factors. Ignoring them would be unwise.

When you are in a ministry for the Lord, it's easy to compare with what similar ministries are doing and gauge your success based on theirs. You may compare yourself on popularity, size of congregation, number of followers, book sales, house size, or the fact they were able to pray over a certain celebrity! The most important thing to focus on when you are in ministry is if you are being faithful to what God is calling you to do; nothing else matters besides obedience. Comparing yourself to someone else in a way that creates discontentment is coveting.

You have no idea the struggles someone else faced to get where they are, you do not know if they are fully moving in God's calling or in their fleshly endeavors, and you do not see behind the scenes of any frustrations, sins, or stress that they conveniently hide behind a pulpit. It is not honoring to God when you are discontent with where He has placed you. That does not mean that you cannot grow, but it does mean that you need to wait on God's timing and be so aligned with His voice that, when He says "move," you move!

CHAPTER 10 REFLECTION AND DISCUSSION QUESTIONS

1. What has been the difference in your life when you used discernment for a career choice vs. not using discernment?

2. What is your motivation to go to work? Why do you keep doing it?

3. What positive or negative examples have you seen in your life regarding working "as unto the Lord"?

4. In what specific ways is your work a battleground, and how can you take ground for Jesus in it?

5. How do ethics apply in your career? Where do you see positive and negative examples of business ethics around you?

6. How do you find balance between your family and career? When has there been a time when one struggled because the other one was a priority?

7. If you are in ministry, how can you find a balance between doing work for Jesus without getting burned out? If you are not in ministry, how can you support those that are?

CHAPTER 11:
DISCERNMENT IN
ENTERTAINMENT MEDIA

The ease of accessibility and amount of content in the media feels like it has grown exponentially in my lifetime alone. Almost any movie, TV show, videogame, or song that you would want is instantly accessible. There is now an easier access to virtual reality so that you can "escape" from your current surroundings. There are very little to no filters on what content you can view unless you put them on yourself.

Ratings on digital content exist but are rarely enforced, allowing any child with knowledge of what buttons to press on his or her parent's smart device to be able to access adult material. Mature content keeps pushing the boundaries for what is acceptable in movies, video games, and TV shows. Content that you would have never seen in the past outside of an adult theater is available for viewing inside the convenience of your own home. How is a Christian to have discernment about media and how it relates to your relationship with God?

SHOW ME THE RULES!

Christians seem to create their own rules on an "individual basis" for what is acceptable to watch or listen to in the media being that there is not a "hard and fast" rule to follow in the Bible. Keep in mind the entertainment industries did not exist when the Bible was written.

We will discuss some guidelines we should follow. I know some Christians that will not watch anything above a 'PG' rating and will not listen to one "major" swear word in any form of media. Other Christians seem to have no filter for the media, allowing anything short of pornography, and yes, many times, even pornography to be seen by their eyes, any type of vulgarity to be heard by their ears, and demonic influences to be entertained by their spirits.

But why have discernment about the media? Why make this a "Christian" issue? It's there for our enjoyment, right?

Let's think about that for a minute. I would hope that most Christians would (should) consider pornography to be inappropriate media to view and rightly so. But why? The answers should be pretty obvious. It is destructive lust that compromises the holy bond God set for a husband and a wife. Jesus said simply looking at a woman with lust is equal to the sin of adultery (Matt. 5:28). By agreeing on this, there is already some sort of guideline established that not *all* entertainment media is okay to view as a Christian.

You may think, "Well, of course, I won't look at pornography, but we're just talking about harmless cable TV shows that are designed to entertain." I would caution you about that thinking in the hope that you understand that the lines between the two are more and more blurred with each passing year. Paul writes to the Corinthian Church about the dangers of using our "freedom" as Christians to justify our actions that do not bring honor to God.

> *Just because something is technically legal doesn't mean that it's spiritually appropriate. If I went around doing whatever I thought I could get by with, I'd be a slave to my whims (1 Cor. 6:12, MSG).*

This verse also extinguishes the argument posed by many to justify inappropriate media consumption that what you see in media is not real, it's just there for entertainment, or it's nothing that you don't hear already at work or school. It's not like you are actually doing or saying those things...

I hope to briefly explore some general guidelines to help aid in your discernment of the entertainment industry. The decisions you make are between you and the Lord and will depend on the stage of your Christian walk and level of Holy-Spirit conviction about these topics.

WHATEVER IS PURE

I believe the best verse to consider as a Christian regarding entertainment is Philippians 4:8:

> *Finally, brothers and sisters, whatever is true, whatever is noble, whatever is right, whatever is pure, whatever is lovely, whatever is admirable- if anything is excellent or praiseworthy- think about such things.*

The Greek word for think, *logizomai,* means to "dwell on, to think in a detailed or logical manner." Controlling your thoughts to be positive and pure 100% of the time seems impossible. Just by watching the news, you will come across stories that disturb your very soul. Even the interactions you have with people at work or the conversations you hear others discussing may not fall into the "positive and pure" category of thought. I believe the goal of this verse is to have discipline in how we think and what we think about. We live in the world, but we do not need to be of the world (John 17:14).

Christians fall into the trap of a *consumerism* mentality that is prevalent in society. Any customer that buys various forms of entertainment media is called a "consumer" for a reason. You take in the content that media provides with your eyes and ears and into your very spirit. Our thoughts and actions are often a by-product of what we consume.

It's not any different when we eat food. If we eat junk food all the time, there will be adverse health and mental effects on our body. The same is true of the media. If there are no limits on the quantity and quality of media you are taking into your body, the output will be adverse effects on your spiritual and even your physical life.

We are cautioned in the Bible to not let "unwholesome talk" come out of our mouths (Eph. 4:29) and that we are defiled by what comes out of our mouths (Matt. 15:11). If we "set our minds on things above, not on earthly things" (Col. 3:2), we should be focusing our time on things that edify us and not the garbage that the flesh and the world provide. Many times, what comes out of our mouths is a natural byproduct of what types of content we are consuming, both good and bad!

I am not trying to paint with a broad brush that *all* entertainment media is negative. There are many different forms that produce encouraging, uplifting, and edifying content. There is not only great Christian music and movies but also positive ones that are not necessarily "Christian" that still showcase good values. A lot of the media I would not even classify as "good" or "bad." It is just there as a choice for entertainment, it is a hobby for many, and it can be an activity that brings people and families together. Many people, including myself, find that watching a movie or playing a videogame is a great way to decompress after a stressful day.

The important thing to understand with entertainment media is that it is a *choice* on what we put in front of our eyes. We should see things from God's perspective as we are being renewed and transformed. A good rule of thumb I heard growing up was "would you watch that if Jesus were in the room?" This is an adequate rule; however, if Jesus was physically in the room, I would probably not watch anything but spend the time talking with Him! Yet Jesus *is* in the room. He is everywhere, omnipresent. We should not forget that obvious but often overlooked fact.

AFFECTS AND EFFECTS

It is important to have discernment about what you personally should or should not watch in regard to how it affects your actions. Some examples to consider would be: someone who curses more after being exposed to movies or music with excessive profanity, a recovering alcoholic having temptations to pick up the habit again after watching a movie with drinking in it, and a man who struggles with lust having uncontrolled thoughts after watching a movie with lots of bikini-clad women in it. These are examples that show there is not always a hard and fast rule for everyone. You need to be aware of how the media affects your thoughts and actions and if you are faced with more temptation after engaging with it.

My wife is an example in how she uses discernment with the types of media she watches, specifically violence. When we were dating, I showed her a scary movie, not just scary but gory scary, not even one I would watch today. This was a terrible mistake. She gets very disturbed in her spirit by this type of violence to the point where it affects her sleep. The same happened when we watched a crime scene investigation show on TV, one with no real "mature" content like profanity or nudity. Now, I know better than to suggest watching these types of shows with her, and she is aware enough of her self-imposed boundaries when it comes to this content that she will not seek it out.

LIMITED TIME

Another factor to consider in having discernment with the entertainment you consume is how much time are you willing to give to it? Your time given to media results in relaxation, engagement, and/or entertainment, but it is always at a cost. I discussed opportunity costs in the chapter on discernment with your time. An opportunity cost is associated with what you are giving up by making a decision.

The opportunity cost in consuming entertainment media is that we give up something else we could do in its place. Even when you multi-task, for example, in the car, you may be listening to music while driving, but the opportunity cost is that you may not be spending time in prayer or listening to the Bible being read to you. Opportunity cost is not always a matter of right or wrong; it just is the consequences of choice.

It becomes a question of priorities when you easily consume a three-hour movie or binge watch a TV show for hours on end but fail to "find" the time to read the Bible or pray. Do you see the disconnect? I have been guilty of the same thing. Media is designed, like advertising, to get your money and your time. Movies are judged by how much money they make at the box office when determining if they are a success. Other media services, like streaming and cable, know that, once they have your time and commitment to a subscription, they then have their hooks in you for future sequels, for word of mouth to your friends, and ultimately, your pocketbook.

Francis Chan, in the book *Crazy Love*, says "I don't want Him [Jesus] to return and find me sitting in a theater."[1] This quote speaks to the fact that there is so much to do for God's Kingdom during the little time we have on Earth that we should not be overly consumed with trying to pass the time and be entertained. Don't get me wrong, I love a good movie as much as anyone. However, using Holy-Spirit-led discernment, I understand that I need to find a good balance and not neglect the most significant parts about our temporal lives, which is our relationship with Jesus Christ and living out the Great Commission.

THINK OF THE CHILDREN

Discernment as a Christian regarding media consumption becomes a more serious topic when dealing with what our minor children should or should not watch. The age of exposure for more and more mature content is unfortunately becoming younger and younger due to the ease of access with smart phones and computers. Children will also make poor decisions when they have access to something that is seen as "off limits" or "adult" in nature because of the thrill they get by acting older than their age, not realizing the harmful effects that are taking place.

This is a topic I have been passionate about. While I was getting my bachelor's degree at Arizona State, I wrote my honors thesis called "Marketing Mature Entertainment to Minors." In it, I tried to find out if there was a direct correlation with big companies trying to market their mature content (R-rated movies, MA-rated videogames, and explicit music) to minors who technically were below the recommended age ratings for purchase. I spent time analyzing if there was actually any clinical evidence to support that consuming mature content actually had a negative effect on the actions taken by those consuming it (ex: playing violent video games makes someone a killer).

In short, while there was no direct correlation based on clinical study (at the time) to support that mature content has a direct influence on someone's actions, I did propose that parents should be held accountable for what media their children consume. Although something like violent video games does not "make" someone turn into a serial killer, for example, it can be a factor along with hundreds of others that influence a person's actions. It may not lead to something drastic, but it could lead to an overall maturing of your children before they are emotionally ready or create a worldview in their minds that is not realistic.

Parents should be the guardians of what is allowed to enter into their children's lives and the same goes for digital content. There are always extreme ends of the spectrum for how people respond to things. It's important to know the individuality of your children to understand if something is going to affect their spirits or cause them to be disturbed.

Since I wrote my thesis in college, analyzing updated and current clinical trials and studies is beyond the scope of this book, but it is important to note that video game addiction has been classified as a "gaming disorder" by the World Health Organization. They describe is as follows:

> Gaming disorder is defined in the 11th Revision of the International Classification of Diseases (ICD-11) as a pattern of gaming behavior ("digital-gaming" or "video-gaming") characterized by impaired control over gaming, increasing priority given to gaming over other activities to the extent that gaming takes precedence over other interests and daily activities, and continuation or escalation of gaming despite the occurrence of negative consequences.
>
> For gaming disorder to be diagnosed, the behaviour pattern must be of sufficient severity to result in significant impairment in

personal, family, social, educational, occu-
pational or other important areas of func-
tioning and would normally have been evi-
dent for at least 12 months.[2]

Even from a secular standpoint, there is a direct effect that media can have on children and adults when discernment is not used in how they consume entertainment.

FREE TO PLAY

Addiction with entertainment, specifically video games, is more fueled now than when I was a child due to the easy accessibility and mobility that is out there. When I was young, it was limited to a movie theater, arcade, or a specific room in my house. The types of portable gaming options available back then were either low quality or had low battery life. Now, minors have almost unlimited accessibility to any movie, video game, streaming, or music options they want "thanks" to their smart phones.

Many companies that release mobile games rely on addiction to fulfill their business model and generate revenue. Notifications remind the owner of a smart phone that it is time to check back with the game, that a new quest is available, or he has received a new message from a friend.

Even in my adult life, shortly after I was married, I played a mobile game that took too much of my time.

It was very addictive to the point that I did not immediately realize how it was affecting me. The goal was to build up your castle and troops in a medieval setting. You could form guilds with up to 100 other players and try to compete for the top rankings in that world. There were positions of authority to be held in the guild and for a period of time, I was in the top position. I had to be in charge of hiring, firing, setting rules, leading raids, and defending.

To stay competitive, it required an increasing amount of time...and money. My wife was more than patient with me during this phase, but I could tell that she was getting frustrated (justifiably) with this game that was consuming my time. The final straw was when I had to pull over the car one time while driving because my castle was getting attacked, which was not a proud moment for me. Once I came to my senses, I deleted this game off my phone.

Why do I tell you this now? Because video games that can be addictive for adults can absolutely be addictive for minor children who have on-the-go access anywhere with their handheld devices. Companies know what sells, and they rely on capturing impressionable minds as new customers. There are many stories in the news of kids who spent thousands of dollars on in-game purchases because their parents did not put limits on their phones and the kids may or may not have realized what was happening.

Children have a "monkey see, monkey do" reaction to things. If you play with a baby for a small amount of time, you will find it starts to mimic what you do. Children have the propensity to act out on what they see in the media because their brains are not fully formed yet. They cannot fully process from a mature perspective what they are seeing. They cannot often discern the difference between fiction and reality. They may act on the words they hear and the actions they see when given the opportunity because it looks or sounds cool to them or they are just curious.

Parents will often justify what their kids see by saying, "Well, they will hear those words anyway in school" or "I can't shelter them forever." While that might be true, why does that mean you should invite it into your home? Shouldn't there be an *example* set so that when they do hear or see something that is wrong, they can combat it with righteousness and knowledge of the Bible?

Even the secular system incorporates ratings of media to help inform parents on what types of content should be limited. There is a difference even in the world's eyes on content that is okay for everyone, for teens and above, and then for mature audiences! Parents that take their *young* children to rated R-movies are doing them a disservice and not using discernment.

I remember growing up watching John Wayne movies as a young kid. They are mild in comparison to much of the content out there today, but even at a young age, I remember certain scenes that seemed to stay "burned" into my memory at the time. The same is true of a very hard game I played by Nintendo. Not being able to beat the final level caused me so much stress that I was having nightmares to the point that my mom had to keep me from playing it!

Children just cannot process and cannot discern the difference between real and fake the way an adult can. Their spirits are growing, and they are susceptible to attacks from the enemy or evil spirits that are allowed to enter their space. Remember that we fight, not against flesh and blood but against spiritual forces of evil (Eph. 6:12).

Parents need to have discernment in not only what they are watching but also what their kids are being exposed to. Parents need to be involved. Ask your kids questions about their emotions after seeing a particular movie, what activities they engage in online, and what the new "craze" is that kids are obsessed with. It's easy to monitor their physical friends but not as easy to monitor their online "friends." Put restrictions in place on their phones or download an app to help monitor their activity, if not for their mental development, then for their physical safety (a topic for another day).

I pray this chapter has not made you defensive but has helped you see the need to guard your senses against things that do not edify you as a Christian, that there is a time and a place for media consumption but that it should be balanced and used with discernment. Saying "I can handle it" is a moot point. "Should you handle it?" is a better question. Find that balance between what you want to do and what you should do. Ask the Holy Spirit for conviction in order to help grow your walk with the Lord.

CHAPTER 11 REFLECTION AND DISCUSSION QUESTIONS

1. How have you seen entertainment media change from when you were growing up?

2. What personal boundaries do you have with entertainment as far as what you do or do not engage with? What caused you to have these boundaries?

3. How can Christians refrain from engaging in a "consumerism mentality" when there is always a new movie, show, video game, or album to consume?

4. In what ways can you engage with positive and pure forms of media? What do those look like for both you and your family?

5. How have you ever been negatively affected by something you watched or listened to in entertainment media? How have you ever been positively affected?

6. How is time a factor for you in relation to what you consume in entertainment?

7. What safeguards do you have or should you have in relation to what your children watch or listen to?

CHAPTER 12:
DISCERNMENT IN SOCIAL MEDIA

Technological breakthroughs have allowed for the once nonexistent and now flourishing use of social media in the culture. The need for people to be connected and to feel like they are a part of something bigger than themselves has fueled social media's popularity. What started as an outlet for college students to stay connected has skyrocketed worldwide into a multi-billion-dollar industry to the point where many phone calls and emails get replaced in favor of using social media. People now relay their most important and private information in semi-public status updates.

Social media allows families to stay connected, long lost relationships to be rekindled, friends to encourage one another, new romances to blossom, businesses to thrive, and career expanding opportunities to be pursued.

However, for every good story of social media's benefits, there seems to be a story of it being used for evil. People can use social media to bully the weak, spread lies, commit predatory actions against children, connect to someone who wants to make it easy to commit adultery, and scam someone out of his money.

Christians are in a new age where utilizing discernment in their social media usage is an important skill to refine in their journey of growing and walking with the Lord. It is important to be aware of the dangers and guard against them.

VALIDATION

Social media has an addictive quality that is hard to ignore. It creates a need to keep checking on it by bombarding you with persistent notifications and a fear of not wanting to "miss out" on what is going on in the news and with your friends. Users of social media can be pushed to the point of compulsion, having to check it frequently throughout the day, facing withdrawal-like symptoms when they don't have access to it.

People receive validation in their minds when a new post is liked, commented on, or shared and when their account gets new followers, friends, messages, waves, tags, or mentions. Social media helps introverts make friends and extroverts gain an increased social status and following.

The validation people get on social media also has a flip side when you compare yourself to others. Social media can cause depression through a dangerous intertwining of envy and covetousness. If you judge your worth by the number of likes a post has or the number of "friends" you have, what happens when those numbers don't add up to where you think they should in your mind? The result can be discontentment which leads to depression.

Craig Groeschel has a terrific book on the topic of social media usage called *Liking Jesus.* In it, he says:

> *The odd thing is the more we focus on ourselves, the less satisfied we feel. And the more we're consumed with the things of this earth, the more we feel empty. The reason is that we were created for more— much more. We were created not for earth but for eternity. We were created not to be Liked but to show love. We were created not to draw attention to ourselves but to give glory to God. We were created not to collect followers but to follow Christ.*[1]

By judging your worth on social media, you start to think that there is something wrong with you, that you are missing out on things, and that you just got a bad roll of the dice in this life. Questions start swirling in your mind. Why does "so and so" have more "friends" than I do? Why did my new post get less likes than my friend's? Why is that couple happier than we are? Why are their kids so well-behaved? How does he get so many vacations? How can they afford that new car? Why did she get such a great job that she loves so much? Why isn't my wife as pretty? Why isn't my husband as fit as hers? The list goes on and on...

If you compare yourself to anyone else, you will always find things that he or she has that you do not. Social media statuses and posts are simply smoke and mirrors. You see the best of people every day; you don't see the husband and wife arguing, the kids screaming, and the pets destroying the furniture. You see people with make-up on, in fancy clothes, in exotic places, living their "best lives" now. Rarely do you see the hurt, the fears, the depression, the anger, and the sadness that the same people hide behind their pictures. You may know nothing of the pain and struggle someone went through to get to where she is today, what she had to do in business to afford what she has, how she damaged her body to look like she does. Everything has a cost associated with it. Everyone is on a journey; his or her starting and finishing points are usually not obvious to others.

One of the Ten Commandments is to not covet (Ex. 20:17). The Hebrew word for covet is *hamad,* meaning "strongly desiring another's possessions." Desiring anything that you do not have, especially to the point of obsession, creates discontentment, anger, jealousy, and rage, which are usually taken out on those around you. Coveting is frequently the starting point that leads to other sins.

James 4:1-3 (MSG) cautions on this as well:

> *Where do you think all these appalling wars and quarrels come from? Do you think they just happen? Think again. They come about because you want your own way, and fight for it deep inside yourselves. You lust for what you don't have and are willing to kill to get it. You want what isn't yours and will risk violence to get your hands on it.*
>
> *You wouldn't think of just asking God for it, would you? And why not? Because you know you'd be asking for what you have no right to. You're spoiled children, each wanting your own way.*

Christians who focus on what they do *not* have cannot be thankful for what they *do* have. Thankfulness and covetousness cannot coexist. Coveting is rarely an outward expression. Coveting starts in the mind, and many times, the actions that *are* seen (anger, depression, sadness, etc.) are simply a byproduct of the battle happening in your thoughts.

Jesus changed the standard for murder and adultery with His sermon on the mount when he instructed that even thinking these thoughts is identical to acting them out (Matt. 5:21-30). Our mind is a battleground; we need to have discernment on how to keep our minds in check with the Holy Spirit.

Paul encouraged the Corinthian Church to "take captive every thought to make it obedient to Christ"

(2 Cor. 10:5b). If social media causes you to sin by negatively influencing your thought life, practice allowing the Holy Spirit to help control your thoughts and speak Scripture in that moment to remind you of God's faithfulness and goodness in your life. We are called to "give thanks in all circumstances; for this is God's will for you in Christ Jesus" (1 Thess. 5:18).

Christians like to quote Philippians 4:13, "I can do all this through him who gives me strength" and rightly so; it's a great verse. The problem comes when they apply it to any situation they want and expect God to give them the strength for it without asking for His will. If you take the verse in context, right before verse 13, Paul is discussing being content in any situation and relying on God for the strength to not want (covet) what you do not have but to be thankful in all things. Here's the whole passage:

> I know what it is to be in need, and I know what it is to have plenty. I have learned the secret of being content in any and every situation, whether well fed or hungry, whether living in plenty or in want. I can do all this through him who gives me strength (Phil. 4:12-13).

NOT SO FAST

I know many Christians that have given up on social media altogether or taken long breaks as a "fast" just so they can focus and "drown out the noise." These are noble actions that are a personal choice and require God-given discernment.

I felt the same thing where I was ready to give up social media due to the amount of time it was consuming and overall negativity I would feel after scrolling through various posts. It seemed like I would see nothing but arguments over a social issue or news stories about heinous acts of sin that occurred all over the world.

One of the reasons I started Discerning Dad was that I felt God telling me that I needed to do something positive about the negativity I was seeing. While I cannot change everything, I thought maybe I could interject some positive focuses on Jesus through my writings or postings. This does not mean I don't still get distracted by the latest "cat video," but it does mean that I found a way to contribute something, however small, to the problem I identified.

If you find yourself being negatively influenced by social media where it is affecting your spiritual walk, go before God and ask if you need to take what the world would consider a "drastic" step and give up social media, maybe for a season. Jesus did use the extreme to make a point when He explained "if your eye causes you to stumble, gouge it out and throw it away. It is better for you to enter life with one eye than to have two eyes and be thrown into the fire of hell" (Matt. 18:9).

Ask yourself, "Could I give up social media if I needed to?" "Do I feel anxiety when I don't check social media?" "What is social media keeping me from doing, and do I feel better or worse after I check it?" These questions can help propel your ability to have discernment when it comes to the social media in your life.

SCREEN TIME

Some calculations estimate the average social media usage per person is two hours per day! That would be more than five years over the course of a lifetime spent on social media! This doesn't even consider the amount of influence social media has on you throughout the day. Two hours of use, for example, would be possibly hundreds of small checks throughout the day, not a two-hour chunk of time. Do you ever pay attention to people when you are out? It's fascinating how many are consumed by their phones, many of which are on social media.

Social media, whether used for good or not, can distract you from using your time on something else. We previously discussed opportunity cost; the opportunity cost of using social media is what you are giving up to be on there. Let's be honest, even if you are "multi-tasking" and doing something else, your time is divided. When I look at social media while my wife is talking to me, I rarely remember what she said, much to her justified frustration!

People can be addicted to social media just like any drug. A high is created by seeing something you like or getting a positive notification, and you go through withdrawals when you are away from it for too long. The problem is, most of the time, people who are addicted to social media don't even realize it's a problem. It's justified by being a "way of life" or "how people function" in the 21st century.

Some discerning questions for inward reflection you can ask yourself regarding social media usage are:

- What is my daily screen time, and what is my goal? (there are apps to help you find this)

- Why are my main goals for getting on social media? (Business, connection, relaxation, information)

- What am I giving up in favor of being on social media? (prayer, family, work, hobbies, etc.)

TROLLING

The Internet has created the ability for people to hide behind their anonymity and act in ways they would never act face to face with someone. People will post things just to cause controversy, to gain attention, to segregate a community, or to blatantly be mean to someone. There are no repercussions to these actions because of the ability to "hide" behind a username or a fake profile. Even with profiles that are real, the users can hide simply because they are communicating digitally and not in the flesh. This creates an avenue for bullies to rise, harsh words to be spoken, and inappropriate content to be viewed whether you want to see it or not.

Christians are not impervious to the temptation to post things online that tear down instead of build up. We have "bolder" than ever Christians online who will not befriend their neighbors or talk to someone at church but *will* be the first person to tell someone online that his doctrine is wrong or he is living in sin!

Before you post anything, first of all, realize that everything you do online, even what you consider to be private, can be accessed and made public. Once it is released, even if you delete it, someone can take a picture and save it. A post can be used against you decades down the road (just take a look at politicians and celebrities).

Christians need to have discernment in how they are portraying Christ in their social media usage. This does not mean that trivial, funny, or random things cannot be posted for a laugh. It does not mean that everything you post or say online has to be biblically related. It does mean that you should not hurt your witness for Christ online because both believers and unbelievers will read what you have to say. Your witness is instantly lost when you resort to immature actions such as name-calling or acting superior to someone else. There is a time and a place for constructive conversation, doctrinal engagement, and differences of opinion. These can all be handled maturely without resorting to harsh words and emotions.

ALL GLORY TO GOD

We do have a guideline in the Bible as Christians with our actions. "Whatever you do, do it all for the glory of God" (1 Cor. 10:31). We should not seek glory for ourselves. We do not need to be "right" simply for the sake of being right and winning an argument. People are not saved through a social media argument; you cannot win someone over with facts but with love.

> We love because he first loved us. Whoever claims to love God yet hates a brother or sister is a liar. For whoever does not love their brother and sister, whom they have seen, cannot love God, whom they have not seen" (1 John 4:19-20).

Just because something is true does not mean it needs to be expressed. John Stott said, "Truth becomes hard if it is not softened by love; love becomes soft if it is not strengthened with truth."[2] Truth and love go hand in hand. The Bible tells us, "Hatred stirs up conflict, but love covers over all wrongs" (Prov. 10:12). Your ability to act in love is *not* dependent on the other person showing you love.

If someone were to pull up your social media postings and interactions ten years from now, would you be proud of them? Would you want your pastor, wife, friends, or children to read them? I know that sometimes I see posts that I made when I first signed up for social media, and they are now embarrassing. For some reason, I felt the need to post frequently about political issues (something I don't do today).

It takes discernment to know how to proceed with hot button topics, social justice issues, and politics. It's not a bad idea to avoid them altogether. A lot of times, these conversations simply escalate to the point where someone says something he or she regrets or gets "unfriended" or blocked. You will not change the culture through your use of social media, but you may change one life by your witness and testimony.

If you choose to continue with social media usage, maybe God has more for you in how you use it. I have found a great number of ministries out there doing the work of the Lord simply by being on social media. Social media allows those ministries to connect on a new level never thought possible in the past. There are great groups out there of godly men and women that you can join. These groups can be there to strengthen and encourage you in your walk with the Lord.

Social media is used as a vessel for prayer as well. God works through prayer requests seen online; struggling believers who have no one to turn to can have an army of Christians ready to pray at a moment's notice when trials and tribulations hit. However, it's important to remember, if you say you are going to pray for someone, not to say you are "praying" without actually interceding to the Father for him or her!

Like most things, it's important to find the right balance when using social media. While not all negative, there are a lot of dangers that we discussed with its usage. It's important to remember that social media might connect people to you that you would never have connected to in real life and that those connections might ultimately lead them to Jesus. The seeds can still be planted in the right way all for God's glory and honor!

CHAPTER 12 REFLECTION AND DISCUSSION QUESTIONS

1. What are some of your general thoughts on how social media has grown over the past decade and how it affects the culture?

2. In what ways do you or others seek validation from social media? What are the dangers of this?

3. How can social media cause you to become discontented with what God has given you?

4. Have you ever given up social media for a period of time or known someone that has? What was the positive or negative impact of this fast?

5. What are some positive ways that social media can be used? How should Christians act on social media?

6. Is there a benefit to heated discussions on social media regarding politics, religion, or another hot button topic? Why is it hard for some people to disengage in these when they wouldn't discuss them in person?

CONCLUSION: DISCERNING STEPS FOR YOUR FUTURE

Chances are that you have read through this book and realized some of the poor choices in areas of discernment you have made in life. Brother or sister, that is okay! I realized the same thing as I wrote this book. Remember we are in a race, not a sprint. No one exercises 100% accurate discernment all the time. Sometimes, our bad choices have little to no consequences, and sometimes, the lack of discernment in major decisions leads to consequences that have to be walked out the rest of your life.

We have the confidence that "if we confess our sins, he is faithful and just and will forgive us our sins and purify us from all unrighteousness" (1 John 1:9). God's grace covers our sins; we then need to make it our goal to move forward and "go and sin no more" as Jesus told the woman caught in adultery (John 8:11).

There may be areas where your lack of discernment has led to hardship and pain in your life. You can think back to those decisions and be paralyzed with fear of making the wrong choices again (ex: marriage). Maybe they weren't even your choices (ex: abuse). They could have been out of your control, but still, you blame yourself.

Your past does not determine your future; give your past over to God. If there is someone you hurt that needs a heartfelt, God-directed apology from you, give it. If there is someone that hurt you in the past but you haven't forgiven him or her, do it. Not for his or her sake but for your own. Unforgiveness leads to bitterness; the bitter root grows as mentioned in Hebrews 12:15 and causes problems in your life and in lives of those around you.

FILL UP

Growing in discernment takes practice like any skill you want to master. You may be gifted in discernment, or it may be something that you need to focus on exercising. Having a relationship with Jesus is key to this growth.

We need both the *logos* and *rhema*, two words used in Greek to describe the Word of God. The *logos* refers to the written Word of God, the Bible. "Let the word *[logos]* of Christ dwell in you richly" (Col. 3:16, KJV). The *rhema* Word of God is God speaking to us personally, communing with our spirit. "Jesus answered:

'It is written,' "Man shall not live by bread alone, but on every word *(rhema)* that comes from the mouth of God"'" (Matt. 4:4). The Bible is our foundation; our relationship with God will allow Him to move in our lives, to impart specific instruction and direction. The *logos* and *rhema* will never contradict one another; they are, together, the fullness of God's revelation to His creation.

When you have discernment in any area of your life, you must check your choices by asking yourself, "What does the Bible say?" and "What is God saying to me directly?" There are times when God will reveal supernatural discernment to an area of our lives, and other times, we will need to rely on our foundational understanding of the Bible as our guidance.

If God is not filling you up, you're either being filled up with something else or running on empty, neither of which is a good alternative!

FIND A PATH

If you feel lost or frustrated with the past, find a new path; don't stay in a place you know leads to death. God's Word will light the way. "Your word is a lamp for my feet, a light on my path" (Ps. 119:105). Jesus said we must follow the narrow road that leads to life and only a few will find it (Matt. 7:14). If you let the world and your flesh be your guide, you will find yourself on an open, easy road that leads to destruction.

Moving forward requires prayer. Ask God to open doors for you, to heal the pain of the past, to grow in the knowledge of God. Prayer is our connection with God. It does not allow us to ask for a cosmic wish list of items, but it can tune our will into God's. Knowing the heart of our Father allows us to understand just a glimpse of His purposes for us, which are always for our good.

Jesus told us in Luke 11:9-13:

> *"So I say to you: Ask and it will be given to you; seek and you will find; knock and the door will be opened to you. For everyone who asks receives; the one who seeks finds; and the one who knocks, the door will be opened.*
>
> *Which of you fathers, if your son asks for a fish, will give him a snake instead? Or if he asks for an egg, will give him a scorpion? If you then, though you are evil, know how to give good gifts to your children, how much more will your Father in heaven give the Holy Spirit to those who ask him!"*

Jesus makes Himself known to creation but hides the deeper things so that we can seek after Him. If you have children, you know that it is nice to be asked for things. We will give the best to our kids, but we want their hearts to be in a place of submission to our authority. If my child demands something from me, you can pretty much guarantee he or she will not get it! My daughter especially knows how to get to her daddy's heart. If she sweetly asks for something at a store, for example, it's game over. She wins.

James 4:2b-3 says:

> You do not have because you do not ask God. When you ask, you do not receive, because you ask with wrong motives, that you may spend what you get on your pleasures.

Does this make you wonder what you do not have because you do not ask? I'm not talking about that new house or car but being able to be in such a close relationship with the Father that you know without a doubt of the direction He wants you to go and knowing what to ask for. If you have discernment about God's will, your prayers will line up with helping you meet this challenge. For example, if I knew God wanted me to plant a church, my prayers would focus around all the details associated with that endeavor. God would bless those prayers because I am aligned with His will. This is a big difference from praying to win the lottery!

PLAN ON GOD

Christians cannot make their plans and then ask God to bless them. Having discernment sometimes requires you to understand God's will for your situation before you take action.

Proverbs 19:21 says, "Many are the plans in a person's heart, but it is the Lord's purpose that prevails."

Other times, you have a vague idea of where God wants you to go and you need to step out in faith. The heroes of faith of Hebrews 11 were commended for their trust in God despite their circumstances. Many like Abraham, Jacob, Moses, and Gideon caught a glimpse of where to go and what to do but still had to commit in action to see God's promises fulfilled. Discernment will not always allow our paths to be 100% clear, showing us where to go, and free of obstacles. Paul writes to the Corinthian Church about how our knowledge now is not complete. All of our questions will not be answered until we are in eternity with Jesus.

1 Corinthians 13:12 (MSG):

We don't yet see things clearly. We're squinting in a fog, peering through a mist. But it won't be long before the weather clears and the sun shines bright! We'll see it all then, see it all as clearly as God sees us, knowing him directly just as he knows us!

I have found in my life that, sometimes, following God's will simply requires saying "yes!" to opportunities in front of you. These open doors have usually gotten me out of my comfort zone, and they weren't even things I asked for. Many of these have been opportunities to serve in various roles in the church, things I never asked for but, when the choice was presented to me, I said yes to. They ended up being a blessing in disguise that helped my growth as a Christian.

God will challenge you to get you out of your comfort zone if you are listening to Him! God cherishes you; you are created in His image! He wants you to grow in your relationship together. He is not content with you to simply "show up" and play church. If you are not moving forward, you are moving backward. We cannot be stagnant in our Christian walk.

Discernment in your life is not just about making the right choice or even the best choice. It is a process of allowing your life to be fully subjected to God and His will, to be a holy example to others, and to grow in the knowledge of Jesus as you move about His purposes and plans for your life until He calls you home. Successful discernment will undoubtedly lead to good consequences and blessings in our lives and those around us; these results should be recognized and used for God's glory and His glory alone!

NOTES

CHAPTER 1

1. Hoomans, Joel. *35,000 decisions: The Great Choices of Strategic Leaders.* 20 March 2015. website. August 2019. <https://go.roberts.edu/leadingedge/the-great-choices-of-strategic-leaders >.

2. Spurgeon, *Charles. Charles Spurgeon on Discernment.* February 2013. 2019.
<https://apologetics315.com/2013/02/charles-spurgeon-on-discernment/>.

3. "Zig Ziglar." Zig Ziglar - *"If You Learn from Defeat, You Haven't Really...,* \
https://www.facebook.com/ZigZiglar/
posts/10152473537212863:0.

CHAPTER 2

1. Manser, Martin H. *The Westminster Collection of Christian Quotations.* Westminster John Knox Press, 2001, p. 22.

2. Donne, John. *John Donnes Devotions upon Emergent Occasions: Together with Deaths Duel.* University of Michigan Press, 1959, pp. 108-109.

3. Sproul, R. C. *Who Is the Holy Spirit?* Reformation Trust Pub., 2012, pp. 30–31.

CHAPTER 3

1. Elliot Ritzema, ed. 300 *Quotations for Preachers.* Bellingham, WA: Lexham Press, 2012.

2. Jones, Curtis. 1000 *Illustrations for Preaching and Teaching.* Nashville, TN: Broadman & Holman Publishers, 1986, p.158.

3. Lee Tan, Paul. *Encyclopedia of 7700 Illustrations: Signs of the Times.* Garland, TX: Bible Communications, Inc., 1996, pp. 407–408.

4. "List of Messiah Claimants." *Wikipedia,* Wikimedia Foundation, 11 Sept. 2019, https://en.wikipedia.org/wiki/List_of_messiah_claimants.

CHAPTER 4

1. Spurgeon, Charles H. *The Complete Works of C. H. Spurgeon, Volume 16: Sermons 788 to 847.* Delmarva Publications, Inc, 2013.

CHAPTER 5

1. Contributors to Wikimedia. "English Real Estate Entrepreneur, Philosopher, Early Quaker and Founder of the Province of Pennsylvania." *Wikiquote,* Wikimedia Foundation, Inc., 11 Apr. 2018, https://en.wikiquote.org/wiki/William_Penn.

2. Twells, Henry. *Hymns and Other Stray Verses.* Wells Gardner, Darton & Co., 1906, p. 34.

CHAPTER 6

1. Huynh, Julie. "Study finds no difference in the amount men and women talk." Undergraduate Biology Research Program, University of Arizona, 19 June 2014, https://ubrp.arizona.edu/study-finds-no-difference-in-the-amount-men-and-women-talk/.

2. Wiersbe, Warren W. *The Bible Exposition Commentary, vol. 2.* Wheaton, IL: Victor Books, 1996, p. 359.

3. Contributors to Wikimedia. "Catholic Saint and Founder of the Franciscan Order." *Wikiquote,* Wikimedia Foundation, Inc., 18 Aug. 2019, https://en.wikiquote.org/wiki/Francis_of_Assisi.

4. Chan, Francis. "How to Argue with Your Spouse." *Desiring God,* 13 Sept. 2019, http://www.desiringgod.org/interviews/

how-to-argue-with-your-spouse.

5. Keefauver, Larry and Judi. *Seventy-Seven Irrefutable Truths of Parenting: Foundations for Godly Parenting.* Orlando, FL: Bridge-Logos, 2001, p. 17.

6. Baker, Warren and Eugene Carpenter. *The Complete Word-Study Dictionary: Old Testament.* AMG Publishers, 2003.

7. Harris, Laird, et al. *Theological Wordbook of the Old Testament.* Moody Publishers, 1980.

CHAPTER 7

1. Lee Tan, Paul. *Encyclopedia of 7700 Illustrations: Signs of the Times.* Garland, TX: Bible Communications, Inc., 1996, p. 827.

2. Green, Michael P. *1500 Illustrations for Biblical Preaching.* Grand Rapids, MI: Baker Books, 2000, p. 249.

3. Elwell, Walter and Barry J. Beitzel. *Baker Encyclopedia of the Bible.* Grand Rapids, MI: Baker Book House, 1988, p. 539.

4. Spurgeon, Charles. *Spurgeon Commentary: Hebrews,* ed. Elliot Ritzema and Jessi Strong, Spurgeon Commentary Series, Bellingham, WA: Lexham Press, 2014, pp.447–448.

CHAPTER 8

1. Stacey Sumereau. "You Don't Have a Soulmate." *Stacey Sumereau,* 26 Feb. 2019, http://www.staceysumereau.com/single-post/2019/02/26/You-Dont-Have-a-Soulmate.

2. Burnes, Jim and Doug Fields. *Getting Ready for Marriage: A Practical Road Map for Your Journey Together.* Colorado Springs, CO: David C Cook, 2014.

3. Chan, Francis and Lisa. *You and Me Forever: Marriage in Light of Eternity.* San Francisco, CA: Claire Love Publishing, 2014.

CHAPTER 9

1. Keefauver, Larry and Judi. *Seventy-Seven Irrefutable Truths of Parenting: Foundations for Godly Parenting.* Orlando, FL: Bridge-Logos, 2001, p. 25.

CHAPTER 10

1. Brand, Chad et al. *Holman Illustrated Bible Dictionary.* Nashville, TN: Holman Bible Publishers, 2003, p. 269.

2. Wagner, C. Peter. *The Church in the Workplace: How Gods People Can Transform Society.* Regal, 2006.

3. Maxwell, John C. *There's No Such Thing as Business Ethics: There's Only One Rule for Making Decisions.* Warner Books, 2003.

4. Evans, Tony. *Kingdom Man: Every Man's Destiny, Every Woman's Dream.* Tyndale House Publishers, 2015.

5. Chandler, Matt. *Work as Worship Retreat 2012* (Right Now, 2012), session 1.

6. Cordeiro, Wayne. *Leading on Empty: Refilling Your Tank and Renewing Your Passion.* Bethany House, 2009.

CHAPTER 11

1. Chan, Francis. *Crazy Love: Overwhelmed by a Relentless God.* David C Cook, 2015.

2. "Gaming Disorder." *World Health Organization,* World Health Organization, 14 Sept. 2018, www.who.int/features/qa/gaming-disorder/en/.

CHAPTER 12

1. Groeschel, Craig. *Liking Jesus: Intimacy and Contentment in a Selfie-Centered World.* Zondervan, 2018, pp. 19-20.

2. Stott, John, *The Message of Ephesians.* Inter-Varsity Press, 1984, p. 172.

Made in the USA
Columbia, SC
24 December 2019

85392160R00130